A NEW
RAILWAY LOCOMOTIVE BOOK

FOR BOYS OF ALL AGES

LOCO'S OF
"THE ROYAL ROAD"

A LINE OF "KINGS"

A NEW RAILWAY LOCOMOTIVE BOOK

FOR BOYS OF ALL AGES

By W. G. CHAPMAN
(*Author of " Cheltenham Flyer," " Track Topics," etc.*)

PUBLISHED IN 1936 BY
THE GREAT WESTERN RAILWAY
(JAMES MILNE, GENERAL MANAGER)
PADDINGTON STATION, LONDON.

REPRINTED IN 1987 BY
DAVID & CHARLES PUBLISHERS PLC

British Library Cataloguing in Publication Data

Chapman, W. G.
  Loco's of "The Royal Road": a new railway
  locomotive book for boys of all ages.
  1. Great Western Railway—History
  2. Locomotive—England—History
  I. Title
  625.2'61'0942   TJ603.4.G72G73

  ISBN 0-7153-8954-8

Originally published by Great Western
Railway in 1936

This composite edition published in 1987
by David & Charles Publishers plc

Printed in Great Britain
by Redwood Burn Limited
Trowbridge   Wiltshire
for David & Charles Publishers plc
Brunel House   Newton Abbot   Devon

Published in the United States of America
by David & Charles Inc
North Pomfret   Vermont 05053   USA

PUBLISHER'S PREFACE

Here is a new printing of one of those immortal classics of the Great Western's publishing activities that helped make the railway perhaps the best known and best loved in the world.

In his *Go Great Western* (to be reprinted), Roger Burdett Wilson wrote: 'August 1923 saw the beginning of a new series of cheap but well illustrated books for railway enthusiasts – young and old. The author was Walter George Chapman, a member of the general manager's staff who joined the Great Western in 1896. In 1908 he was awarded one of the first three I.K. Brunel Medals for the most successful student in the railway department of the London School of Economics. While in the general manager's office he wrote four books in the series "For Boys of All Ages", and after being transferred to the publicity department in 1929 produced three more as well as editing the *Engine Book*. The first title in the series was *The 10.30 Limited*, and as was to be expected, sales of such a well-produced book on such a popular subject, modestly priced at a shilling (5p), were phenomenal. Seventy-one thousand copies were sold in six months, and of the first four Chapman books 130,000 found their way into the hands of grateful "boys of all ages".'

Loco's of the Royal Road was published in 1936 and is reprinted here in association with British Rail Western Region. David & Charles are also reprinting other 'Books for Boys of All Ages', and the 'Engine Book' titled *GWR Engines: Names, Numbers, Types & Classes* (in fact a reprint of several different issues together) has long been a standard item in the David & Charles list, along with many other GWR titles. Send for complete list.

FOREWORD

THIS book owes its title—or the better part of it—to none other than His Majesty King Edward VIII, who (then The Prince of Wales) as the chief guest at a banquet held in celebration of the centenary of the Great Western Railway, graciously referred to the Company's many associations with the Royal House, and honoured the Railway with the name " The Royal Road."

That the locomotive is the most spectacular among a wealth of fascinating features comprising a modern railway system will probably be generally conceded by railway enthusiasts, and certainly by the younger generation. At any rate the statement would appear to be borne out by the fact that two volumes devoted exclusively to Great Western Railway engines—" Caerphilly Castle " (1924) and " The ' King ' of Railway Locomotives " (1928)—have already appeared among the six books hitherto comprising the G.W.R. " Boys of All Ages " series of publications and four large editions of the former and two of the latter (over 60,000 copies) have been exhausted.

Still, the voracious appetite of youth for information upon the subject goes unappeased, and, as the year 1936 marks the centenary of G.W.R. locomotives (for it was in June, 1836 that Brunel started making enquiries for engines for his railway), this new book dealing with a century of locomotive development on the G.W.R., makes its appearance.

It was originally intended to call this seventh volume in the series " From ' North Star ' to the ' Kings '," or, alternatively, " A Century of G.W.R. Locomotives," had not the title adopted been so opportunely supplied. Therefore, " Loco's of ' The Royal Road '—A New Railway Locomotive Book for Boys of All Ages," is submitted with the hope that it may be found worthy of the kindly and critical examination vouchsafed to its predecessors.

Any book of this kind must obviously include a certain amount of information which has been embodied in one, or other, of the preceding volumes on the subject, but in such cases the text has been carefully revised and brought up to date.

In conformity with other volumes in the series, the text is in narrative form and the reader is asked to regard it as a resumption of the talks with the young railway enthusiast of " Cheltenham Flyer " and " Track Topics."

READING, 1936.   W.G.C.

ARRANGEMENT OF TALKS

Talk Number One	INTRODUCTORY	9
Talk Number Two	THE EARLIEST LOCOMOTIVES ..	15
Talk Number Three	" NORTH STAR "	27
Talk Number Four	THE FIRST STANDARD ENGINES ..	41
Talk Number Five	SWINDON TAKES A HAND	47
Talk Number Six	GOOCH'S " EIGHT-FOOT-SINGLES " AND OTHERS	61
Talk Number Seven	1864 TO 1902	75
Talk Number Eight	4–4–0 TO 4–6–0	93
Talk Number Nine	4–6–0'S ESTABLISHED, SUPER-HEATING, ETC.	105
Talk Number Ten	" CASTLES," " HALLS," AND OTHERS	119
Talk Number Eleven	THE MIGHTY " KINGS "	129
Talk Number Twelve	TRACTIVE EFFORT AND CLASSIFICA-TION	145
Talk Number Thirteen	THE ENGINE COMPONENTS ..	159
Talk Number Fourteen	THE BOILER COMPONENTS ..	173
Talk Number Fifteen	CONSTRUCTING THE BOILER ..	183
Talk Number Sixteen	BUILDING THE LOCOMOTIVE ..	193
Talk Number Seventeen	THE WORKING OF THE LOCOMOTIVE	207
Talk Number Eighteen	CONCLUSION	221

TALK NUMBER ONE

INTRODUCTORY

Y OU may be aware that Silver Jubilee year also marked the centenary of the Great Western Railway. The centenary celebrations took the form of a luncheon at Bristol where the Great Western Railway was born, and a banquet in London at which H.R.H. The Prince of Wales (now King Edward VIII) was the principal guest.

A film portraying the chief events in the Great Western Railway's hundred years of existence was produced, and a special Great Western Railway Centenary Supplement was issued by the *Times* newspaper. The occasion was also marked by the introduction of a new express train *The Bristolian* between London and Bristol, the termini of the original Great Western Railway, at timings which placed it second only to the famous *Cheltenham Flyer* for the highest average speed of any train in the G.W.R. timetable.

Whilst much was written and spoken on many and diverse aspects of the undertaking in connection with the celebration of the Railway's hundred years of corporate existence, reference to the happy associations which have so long existed between the company, its staff, and its public, and which for want of a better term may be called " the G.W.R. tradition " ran like a silver thread through all those utterances.

Now this G.W.R. tradition is a very real thing. It is admittedly difficult to define, but it is a compound of various elements, among which prestige and pride of service are considerable. It undoubtedly owes much to such stalwarts as Brunel, Gooch, and Saunders who so auspiciously launched the enterprise a hundred years ago, and it has been nourished by their successors, and (here is my point) has flourished on the performances of G.W.R. locomotives and trains. Few would deny that when referring to the G.W.R. tradition, they have somewhere in their minds, the contribution made by such glorious old timers as *Lord of the Isles* and *Flying Dutchman*, as well as the *Kings* and *Castles* and *Cornish Riviera Limited* and *Cheltenham Flyer* of to-day.

In these times of modern publicity, keen competition, and rapid development it is surely no mean achievement that what is essentially a commercial undertaking should have as part of its very constitution such a priceless and jealously guarded tradition. That it is no new acquisition has been evidenced by many who have had contact with the Company for a long period of years, and we have only to recall the affection shown by a large section of the general public for the old broad gauge, and its attitude in the historic gauge controversy, to furnish one example of the sentiment as it existed forty odd years ago.

You may ask what all this has to do with Great Western Railway locomotives. Well, I should answer that the speed achievements of the Great Western Railway, which were conspicuous from its early days and have done so much for the G.W.R. tradition, have been primarily due to a noble line of locomotives. What is more, I think this must have been in the minds of those responsible for the arrangements in connection with the G.W.R. centenary banquet, for on that historic occasion each guest was given a small souvenir representation of the famous old engine *Lord of the Isles*. That was, indeed, a happy inspiration, for no fitter emblem could have been selected to exemplify the spirit of the Great Western Railway, and what I have haltingly tried to define as the G.W.R. tradition.

"Lord of the Isles."

In this series of talks, I want to tell you roughly in chronological order, and with some diversions, the story of Great Western Railway locomotives over the century 1836—1936 from the small six-wheeled, two-cylinder engines to the giant ten-wheeled four-cylinder locomotives of today. In doing so, you will discover how the *Castles* and *Kings* are the lineal descendants of *North Star* of a century ago.

You already know something of how the locomotive works and how the engines are classified by wheel arrangement, etc., and you have had an opportunity of visiting Swindon Works of the Great Western Railway and seeing for yourself locomotives in course of construction ;* while in our talks about the railway track you were told the story of the conversion of the Great Western Railway's original broad (7 ft.) gauge to standard gauge.† Much of that information will form a useful background for the story of G.W.R. locomotive progress.

After tracing the development of the locomotive to its present stage, we will briefly discuss the various types of engines and their uses. Then I think we might usefully consider the chief components and the building of an engine and its working, by which time you should have amassed as much information about locomotives of " The Royal Road," their functions, construction, and abilities as the most inquisitive young railway enthusiast can be expected to assimilate in the time at our disposal.

---

*See " Cheltenham Flyer."
†See " Track Topics."

" The Bristolian " Express crossing Wharncliffe Viaduct

"Vulcan" (1837)
Built by Chas.
Tayleur & Co.,
Warrington.

The first loco-
motive to run
on The Great
Western Railway

TALK NUMBER TWO

THE EARLIEST LOCOMOTIVES

I N our recent talks on the railway track and its structures, we spoke of the early days of the Great Western Railway and the part played by Isambard Kingdom Brunel, who was Chief Engineer of the undertaking from 1833 to 1859.* From what you know of his energetic personality you will not be surprised to learn that within ten months of Royal Assent being obtained to the Bill authorising the construction of the line between London and Bristol (August 31st, 1835), Brunel was making enquiries for locomotives for his railway.

On June 14th, 1836, writing from 18, Duke Street, Westminster, Brunel addressed letters to certain builders of locomotive engines of that time asking :—

" Whether they would undertake, in what period and upon what terms, to supply two locomotive engines . . . The weight of the engine exclusive of the tender, but in other respects supplied with water and fuel for work, not to exceed $10\frac{1}{2}$ tons, and if above 8 tons, to be carried upon 6 wheels . . . The width in the clear between the rails will be 7 feet, the height of the chimney as usual . . . All the materials and workmanship to be of the very best description and, excepting when modifications may be necessary, to comply with the conditions above stated, or, for the purpose of improvement, to be similar to the same

*See " Track Topics."

15

parts of the best engines now used on the Liverpool and Manchester Railway."

This quotation from the circular letter asking for tenders is an abridged one, and though certain other conditions were imposed and Brunel asked for drawings to be submitted before work was started, he seems to have left the form of construction of the engines very largely in the hands of the builders.

In due course tenders were received and twenty engines ordered from various makers. We have it on the authority of the late Mr. E. L. Ahrons, who had a special knowledge of early G.W.R. locomotive history, that " there never has existed such an extraordinary collection of freak locomotives as these which were built for the Great Western Railway, and delivered during the period of about eighteen months from November, 1837."

But I am afraid we are moving rather too quickly, for on July 18th, 1837, an ambitious young man, who had then not attained his majority*, addressed the following letter of application to Brunel for employment with the Great Western Railway. The original letter still survives and is a treasured possession of the Company. It is headed Manchester and Leeds Railway, Rochdale, where the writer was then temporarily employed with his elder brother.

" I have just been informed it is your intention to erect an Engine Manufactory at or near Bristol and that you wish to engage a person as Manager. I take the earliest opportunity of offering my services for the situation. I have until the last two months been constantly engaged

---

*Gooch was born at Bedlington, Northumberland, on August 24th, 1816.

Facsimile of Gooch's letter of application for employment

in engine building and have worked at each branch of the business, but principally at Locomotive Engine Work. The first three years of my time I was with Mr. Homphry at the Tredegar Iron Works, Monmouthshire. I left him to go to Mr. R. Stephenson and was at the Vulcan

Foundry 12 months when I obtained leave from Mr. Stephenson to go down to Mr. Stirling of the Dundee Foundry Co. Dundee to get a knowledge of steamboat work. I remained with him 12 months and returned to Mr. Stephenson's works at Newcastle where I remained until last October when I left, having had an offer from a party in Newcastle to take the management of a loco-motive manufactory which they intended erecting but which owing to some unavoidable circumstances they have now given up the idea of proceeding with and we have countermanded the order for machinery. This left me without a situation and I am anxious to engage myself to some Company where I will have the management of the building of engines."

The writer of that letter was one Daniel Gooch, who was destined to devote 52 years of his life to Great Western Railway interests, and to become Sir Daniel Gooch, Chairman of the Great Western Railway Company. He may be said to have influenced, more than any other person, the locomotive policy of the Railway.

Young Gooch certainly did not let the grass grow under his feet for, exactly one month after writing to Brunel, he was appointed Locomotive Assistant and took up his duties on August 18th, 1837.

It is interesting to recall that at this time the combined ages of the Chief Engineer and Locomotive Superintendent of the Great Western Railway totalled rather more than 52 years. Verily this was an age in which very young men shouldered very great responsibilities.

At this point we cannot, I think, do better than give an extract from Gooch's reminiscences, for here we have the first hand impressions of the young locomotive engineer regarding that queer assortment of engines which was to become his first charge, as well as the cause of considerable perturbation. Referring to the time of his appointment (August, 1837), he writes :—

" None of the engines had then been delivered, although several were ordered. My first work was to prepare plans for the engine-houses at Paddington and Maidenhead, and then I went to inspect the engines then building. I was not much pleased with the design of the engines ordered. They had very small boilers and cylinders, and very large wheels. Those made by the Vulcan Company had wheels 8 ft. in diameter, and three of them only 12 in. cylinders with 18 in. stroke ; two of Mather Dixon's had 10 ft. wheels and 14 in. cylinders, with very small boilers. Those made by Hawthorne were on a patent plan of Tom Harrison's, having the engine and the boiler on separate carriages, and coupled with ball-and-socket steam pipes.

" These were immense affairs ; the boilers were very large, and cylinders were, I think, 16 in. diameter, and about 2 ft. stroke. In one, the cylinders were coupled direct to the driving wheels, which were 10 ft. diameter, and the other had a spur and pinion 3 to 1, with 6 ft. wheel making the wheel equal to 18 ft. diameter. The same plan of gearing was used in the two engines built by the Haigh Foundry ; their wheels were 6 ft. diameter and the bearing 2 to 1, but the cylinders were small. I felt very uneasy about the working of these machines, feeling sure they would have enough to do to drive themselves along the road."

LOCO'S OF 'THE ROYAL ROAD'

I will not weary you with much in the way of detail with regard to these earliest of Great Western Railway loco-

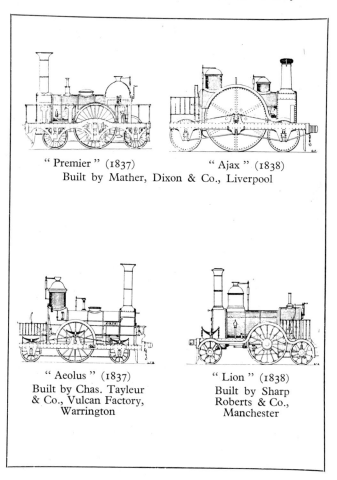

"Premier" (1837)
"Ajax" (1838)
Built by Mather, Dixon & Co., Liverpool

"Aeolus" (1837)
Built by Chas. Tayleur
& Co., Vulcan Factory,
Warrington

"Lion" (1838)
Built by Sharp
Roberts & Co.,
Manchester

motives, but you may like to know that *Vulcan* (Tayleur and Co.) and *Premier* (Mather Dixon & Co.) were the first two delivered—on November 25th, 1837*, having come from Liverpool by sea to London, thence by river and canal to West Drayton, although the railway track was not available for them there until towards the end of December. *Vulcan* had a trial run on December 28th and was thus the first locomotive to run on the Great Western Railway.

North Star (Robert Stephenson & Co.), of which much more anon, was delivered on November 28th, 1837, and had been sea-borne from Newcastle-on-Tyne to London and thence conveyed by barge up the river to Maidenhead, where it had to wait for the rails to reach that point. Delivery of other engines followed at intervals; seventeen being received up to the end of 1838.

The extraordinary engines *Thunderer* and *Hurricane* built by Messrs R. & W. Hawthorn, and referred to by Gooch, were such departures from anything hitherto (or since) seen in the railway locomotive world that I should like to quote what Mr. Ahron said about one of them, i.e., *Thunderer*† :—

"The main feature of the design was the complete separation of the engine from the boiler, each forming an independent vehicle. The whole constituted a sort of procession. First came the engine, the cylinders of which were placed at the back, and the driver took his stand in an exposed position in front of them. The second

---

*This may be date of assembly of parts as Ahron gives delivery date as Nov. 10th.
†History of the Great Western Railway, Vol. 1, Part 2.

vehicle carried the boiler only, which was one of the usual locomotive type with smokebox and chimney in front, conveniently arranged so that the steam and exhaust pipes passed directly from the smokebox end to the cylinders on the first vehicle. The connections were made by means of gland pipes with ball and socket joints at each end. The fireman, who was separated from the driver, stood on a footplate, in the usual place at the rear of the boiler carriage. The third vehicle was an ordinary tender, and finally there came the train " at the back of beyond." One of the objects of the arrangement was to obtain a large boiler, at the same time avoiding excessive weight on the engine wheels, but there was the disadvantage of making the adhesive weight of the engine too small. It was also claimed that the boiler carriage could always be uncoupled when the engine was under repairs, and used with another similar engine or *vice versa*."

Here are illustrations of some of the earliest of Great Western Railway locomotives and it is indeed a pity that authentic illustrations of unique *Thunderer* and *Hurricane* are not available, but these drawings, though not correct in every detail, give a fair idea of what these queer contraptions were like. They were delivered to the Company on March 6th, 1838, and October 5th, 1838, respectively, and both ceased work in December, 1839 ; in fact, they do not seem to have been brought into regular traffic at any time.

You may like to see a list of those early G.W.R. locomotives. It gives a few salient dimensions of each of the engines by the various makers. I have purposely omitted the *Stars* which were in quite another class, and to which I want to devote a separate talk.

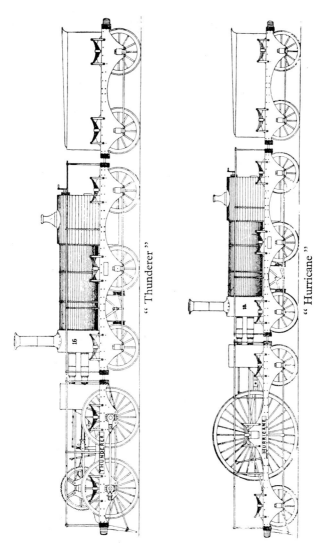

" Thunderer "

" Hurricane "

Built by R. and W. Hawthorn, Newcastle

23

While the Mather Dixon engines had average service lives of less than two years, the Vulcan Foundry engines were in service on the average about $21\frac{1}{2}$ years, and the engines

Name	Cylinders Diam. : Stroke	Diam. of Wheels No.	Diam. of Wheels Drvg.	Diam. of Wheels No.	Diam. of Wheels Carrying	Weights (empty) Engine	Weights (empty) Tender	Date Delivered	Date Ceased Work
MATHER DIXON & CO., LIVERPOOL.									
	ins.		ft.		ft.	T. C.	T. C.		
Premier ..	$14\frac{1}{2} \times 14\frac{1}{2}$	2	7	4	$4\frac{1}{2}$	13 10	5 6	Nov. 25, '37	Dec., '40
Aerial ..	14×14	2	7	4	$4\frac{1}{2}$	13 10	5 6	Mar. 4, '38	Dec., '40
Ajax ..	14×20	2	10	4	5	—	—	Dec. 12, '38	June, '40
Planet ..	16×20	2	8	4	—	—	—	Aug. 1, '39	June, '40
Mercury (No. 1;)	14×18	2	8	4	—	—	—	Sept. 26, '39	Dec., '43
Mars (No. 1)	—	2	8	4	—	—	—	April 20, '40	Dec., '40
TAYLEUR & CO., VULCAN FOUNDRY, WARRINGTON.									
Vulcan ..	14×16	2	8	4	$4\frac{1}{2}$	16 3	5 16	Nov. 25, '37	April, '68
Aeolus ..	14×16	2	8	4	$4\frac{1}{2}$	16 3	5 16	Nov. 30, '37	April, '67
Bacchus ..	14×16	2	8	4	$4\frac{1}{2}$	16 3	5 16	Dec. 2, '37	June, '42
Apollo ..	12×16	2	8	4	$4\frac{1}{2}$	14 13	5 16	Jan. 16, '38	Aug., '67
Neptune ..	12×16	2	8	4	$4\frac{1}{2}$	14 13	5 16	Mar. 5, '38	Dec., '40
Venus (No. 1)	12×16	2	8	4	$4\frac{1}{2}$	14 13	5 16	Sept. 7, '38	July, '70
R. & W. HAWTHORN, NEWCASTLE.									
Thunderer ..	16×20	4	6	{4 {2	$4\frac{1}{2}$ 4	—	—	Mch. 6, '38	Dec., '39
Hurricane ..	16×20	2	10	10	4	—	—	Oct. 6, '38	Dec., '39
SHARP, ROBERTS & CO., MANCHESTER.									
Lion	14×15	2	6	4	$3\frac{1}{2}$	12 $17\frac{1}{2}$	11 4	May 6, '38	June 1847
Atlas	14×15	2	6	4	$3\frac{1}{2}$	12 $17\frac{1}{2}$	11 4	June 6, '38	1872
Eagle	14×15	2	6	4	$3\frac{1}{2}$	—	—	Nov. 8, '38	1871
HAIGH FOUNDRY CO., WIGAN.									
Viper ..	$14\frac{3}{4} \times 18$	2	$6\frac{2}{5}$	4	$3\frac{1}{2}$	—	—	Aug. 30, '38	Jan., '68
Snake ..	$14\frac{3}{4} \times 18$	2	$6\frac{2}{5}$	4	$3\frac{1}{2}$	—	—	Sept. 7, '38	Nov., '69

supplied by Sharp, Roberts & Co. and the Haigh Foundry had working lives of about 25 and 30 years respectively.

You will see from the tables that Brunel's expressed wish in regard to the weights of the engines was not, and probably could not be, complied with.

With regard to the diameter of the driving wheels, Brunel explained, in his evidence before the Gauge Commissioners in 1845, that his original intention was to have driving wheels of 7 ft. or 8 ft. for his passenger locomotives, and that the 10 ft. experiment, for which he took full responsibility, had been suggested by certain of the makers, but did not prove successful.

The fact is that these were the early days of railways, and though at that time there had been considerable development in locomotive construction towards certain types and in such matters as proportional dimensions, etc., Brunel had set his mind on achieving higher speeds than had hitherto been contemplated. Hence his desire for 8 ft. diameter driving wheels when 5 ft. was the usual dimension.

We must remember also that no locomotives had previously been constructed to such dimensions as those which Brunel required to work on his 7 ft. gauge railway.

We hear today a good deal about the question of air resistance on moving vehicles, but it is as old as railway locomotives themselves—or nearly so—for in a letter to Messrs. Tayleur & Co. (Vulcan Foundry) on the subject of supplying the first locomotives to the Great Western Railway, we find Brunel making a suggestion for " a bow or round front to take off the direct action of the air against the flat surface of the smoke-box." So you see, while the term " streamlining " may not have then been thought of, Brunel was aware of the effects of air resistance on moving vehicles a whole century ago.

I don't know if you are astronomically minded, but I think at this juncture we might profitably study the *Stars* for a little while, for if they did not foretell it, they certainly helped to shape the future of G.W.R. locomotives.

"North
Star"—
1837

TALK NUMBER THREE

NORTH STAR

WHEN discussing the earliest of G.W.R. engines, I quoted an authority as stating that " there never has existed such a collection of freak locomotives as those built for the Great Western Railway." Now I particularly want to emphasise the last six words of that quotation, for while *North Star* was one of the earliest engines delivered, she was *not* built for the Great Western Railway.

North Star was constructed by Robert Stephenson & Co. in 1837. The firm had built their first engine of that name for the Liverpool and Manchester Railway seven years before, in fact, the name seems to have been a favourite one with locomotive builders of that time. *North Star* which, as we have seen, was delivered to the Great Western Railway at Maidenhead at the end of November, 1837, was, with a sister engine *Morning Star* (delivered Jan. 24th, 1839) actually constructed to the order of the New Orleans Railway, U.S.A. It is believed that *North Star* was sent out to America but not landed, as financial difficulties had arisen after despatch, or, to quote the words of Robert Stephenson (the builder), " in consequence of the panic which came over the commercial world." *North Star* was returned to the makers and, with *Morning Star*, was lying on their hands until the two locomotives were acquired by Brunel, for the Great Western Railway.

By the way, I believe there is some confusion in the minds of young students of railway history regarding the Stephensons, and I am not altogether surprised, for many loose statements have been made, some in " works of reference," e.g. a popular encyclopædia says that George Stephenson (1781-1848) was the inventor of the locomotive —meaning presumably " steam railway locomotive "— which is a common mis-statement. No one would detract anything from George Stephenson's glorious achievements as " the father of railways," but he built his first loco-motive *Blucher* in 1814 and Richard Trevithick's second locomotive was employed on the Merthyr Tydfil train road ten years *earlier*. After his appointment as Engineer to the Liverpool and Manchester Railway, George Stephenson turned his attention mainly to railway construction and, anticipating a demand for locomotives, a company was

" North Star " as rebuilt in 1854

Reconstructed " North Star "—1925

formed with his son Robert Stephenson (1803-1859) in charge and it was this company (Messrs. Robert Stephenson & Co.), which built the famous " Rocket " (to the joint order of George and Robert Stephenson) and the old *North Star* which we are now discussing.

Robert Stephenson, by the way, was a close friend of Brunel's and the godfather of the Chief Scout and founder of the world-wide Boy Scout and Girl Guide movements. Lord Baden-Powell's full names are Robert Stephenson Smyth Baden-Powell.

That is a little digression, but perhaps it clears the air somewhat. Now we must get on.

When placing the order for *North Star* Brunel, addressing his friend Robert Stephenson, wrote, " I look forward to having such an engine as never before." By the time we have finished talking about *North Star* I think you will agree that Brunel's expectations were fully realised.

G.W.R. Locomotives ancient and modern—"North Star" and "King George V"

As originally constructed *North Star* and *Morning Star* were of 5 ft. 6 ins. gauge with driving wheels of 6 ft. 6 ins. diameter, cylinders 16 ins. diameter and 16 ins. stroke, and fitted with what was known as " Gab " motion. There were two separate safety valves and a dome mounted on the boiler of *North Star* as shown in this photograph. The engine was altered by the makers to Brunel's 7 ft. gauge and *North Star* was fitted with 7 ft. driving wheels.

North Star has been described as of the orthodox design of the period. She was doubtless steamed before the rails had been extended to Maidenhead and her first running trial was made there on May 1st, 1838. Brunel was certainly pleased with *North Star* for, writing to T. E. Harrison (under whose patents *Thunderer* and *Hurricane* were constructed), in March 1838, he said : " We have a splendid engine of Stephenson's ; it would have been a beautiful ornament in the most elegant drawing room."

Gooch also thought well of *North Star* as a result of experience, for in his diary regarding the opening of the section London to Maidenhead he says :

" On 31st May, 1838, the directors made their first trip over the whole length of this portion, and it was opened to the public on the 4th June, and then my difficulties with the engines began. The *North Star* and the six from the Vulcan Foundry Company were the only ones I could at all depend upon. For many weeks my nights were spent in a carriage in the engine-house at Paddington, as repairs had to be done to the engines at night to get them to do their work next day. The *North Star* being the most powerful one and in other respects the best, was my chief reliance, but she was often getting into trouble from other causes."

It is interesting in passing to recall that Gooch, prior to coming to the Great Western Railway, had served with both Robert Stephenson & Co. and the Vulcan Foundry.

On the trip of May 31st, 1838, when *North Star* drew the directors' train containing about 200 passengers, the $22\frac{1}{2}$ miles from Paddington to Maidenhead Bridge (now Taplow) were covered in 47 minutes, or at an average speed of 28 miles an hour. *North Star* also had the honour of hauling the first passenger train on the Great Western Railway when the section Paddington to Maidenhead Bridge was opened to the public on June 4th, 1838.

There is a record in the diary of a G.W.R. director (Mr. G. H. Gibbs) under date December 29th, 1838, which reads :—

" I went to-day to Maidenhead in an experimental train to test Brunel's statements as to the improvement effected in the *North Star*. We carried 43 tons of carriages and load at an average of 38 miles an hour, consuming only 0.95 lbs. of coke per ton of net weight per mile."

The " improvements effected " refers to alteration to the blast pipe made as the result of some experiments by Brunel.

To complete the story of *North Star*, it is now necessary to make a diversion from chronological order in this narrative. In 1854, after having been in service about sixteen years, she was rebuilt with cylinders 16 ins. by 18 ins., Gooch's expansion gear fitted, and the boiler pressure increased from about 50 to 100 lbs. per square inch. The boiler was then extended about 5 ins., the dome

" North Star " taking part in the G.W.R. Centenary Film (1935)

removed, the safety valves combined and placed over the fire-box, and the wheel base extended. In her altered condition *North Star* gave valued service for another sixteen years (till December, 1870) and covered 429,000 miles in 32 years of active work on the Great Western Railway.

North Star was a remarkably successful engine and in her early days was the most, if not one of the most powerful locomotives then extant. It is probably true to say that she had more effect upon subsequent locomotive design in this and other countries than any other engine. She certainly affected the whole line of G.W.R. engines which was to follow her.

The old locomotive was retained at Swindon after her useful life was over, but in 1906, I am sorry to say, owing to lack of space in which to store this old veteran and others, the order had to be given—not without many misgivings you may be sure—for her to be broken up.

Fortunately, however, that is not the end of the story, for, in connection with the railway centenary celebrations held at Darlington in 1925 (to commemorate the opening of the first public railway), it was felt that an effort should be made to reconstruct this famous engine. Certain principal parts, including the crank axle and wheels were discovered at Swindon—doubtless no one had the heart to scrap them—and other of the original components were contributed from various sources when the intention of rebuilding the old locomotive became known. These included the name-plates and one of the buffers, the latter being a treasured souvenir, padded with horsehair, and doing duty as a music stool. It was really extraordinary how many of the original parts were recovered and from how many different sources.

Besides taking part in the 1925 railway centenary celebrations, the rebuilt *North Star* was sent overseas to America in 1927, and on this occasion she was accompanied by the first of the powerful four-cylinder " King " class engines *King George V*. These two engines, representing G.W.R. locomotives ancient and modern, were exhibited at the Baltimore and Ohio Railway Centenary, the " Fair of the Iron Horse." Thus *North Star* made her second trip across " the herring pond " after an interval of ninety years !

The rebuilt *North Star* is still to be seen at Swindon Works. She recently came out of her retirement again in connection with the Great Western Railway centenary celebrations and, on this occasion the old lady went quite gay and blossomed out as a cinema " star." In the film " The Romance of a Railway " she was at the head of a train of old-time railway coaches containing passengers attired in costumes of a century ago, as you see in this photograph.

Thanks to the celluloid medium *North Star* has recently attracted a wide circle of admirers, for members of the staff of the Great Western Railway with their wives and families have been afforded an opportunity of seeing this noble ancestor of the G.W.R. locomotive family " doing her stuff," if such an expression is permissible when talking of a centenarian.

Besides the celebrated old broad-gauger there have been three other *North Stars*, and doubtless succeeding G.W.R locomotive superintendents have been desirous of perpetuating a name which is so worthy of veneration in

Great Western Railway locomotive history. Here is a comparative table of the G.W.R. *North Stars* :—

No.	Builder	Year	Type	Cylinders		Driving Wheels		Boiler Pressure lbs. per sq. in.	Heating area sq. ft.	Grate area sq. ft.	Remarks
				No.	ins.	No.	Dia. ft. in.				
—	R. Stephenson & Co., Newcastle-on-Tyne	1837	2-2-2	2	16 ×16	2	7 0	50	711	—	Rebuilt 1854
380	G.W.R., Swindon (Armstrong)	1866	2-2-2	2	17 ×24	2	7 0	120	1269	16.75	Converted in 1902 to 0-6-0 with 5ft. driving wheels
3072	G.W.R., Swindon (Dean)	1894	4-2-2	2	19 ×24	2	7 8	160	1561	—	
40	G.W.R., Swindon (Churchward)	1906	4-4-2	4	14¼ ×26	4	6 8½	225	2143	27.07	Rebuilt as 4-6-0 1909. Rebuilt as a "Castle," 1929.

Although this talk is intended to be primarily about *North Star*, I ought to mention that *Morning Star* differed from her sister engine only in small details of design as you can see from this drawing, but she retained her original 6 ft. 6 ins. driving wheels.

North Star weighed 18 tons 15 cwts. and *Morning Star* probably somewhat less owing to her smaller driving wheels, but both these weights were well in excess of Brunel's original estimate of 10½ tons as the maximum for a six-wheeled engine.

Before closing this talk I ought to add that, as *North Star* and *Morning Star* were the only really reliable engines acquired by the Company in its earliest days, ten more *Stars* were ordered from Messrs R. Stephenson & Co., and of

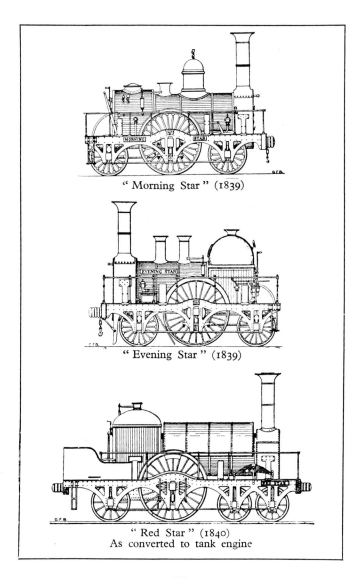

" Morning Star " (1839)

" Evening Star " (1839)

" Red Star " (1840)
As converted to tank engine

these, *Evening Star* and *Dog Star*, were delivered in 1839 and the remainder in 1840-41.

Generally speaking these engines were similar in design to *North Star*. They had 7 ft. driving wheels, and 4 ft. carrying, (leading and trailing) wheels, as had all the *Stars* of that period, but the cylinder dimensions were somewhat increased.

Polar Star and *Red Star* were the next two to come into service, and they started work in July and August, 1840, respectively. You will probably be surprised to hear that these were the first two locomotives to have flanged driving wheels. Accustomed as we are to-day to the flanged driving wheel, it is not a little surprising to learn that the driving wheels of G.W.R. locomotives prior to that time were flangeless.

And here we leave the *Stars* in their courses to consider, in our next talk, the first G.W.R. standard locomotives.

" North Star " and train of old-time coaches in the G.W.R. Centenary Film (1935)

"Firefly" (1840)
Built by Jones,
Turner, and
Evans, Newton,
Lancs.

TALK NUMBER FOUR

THE FIRST STANDARD ENGINES

A LTHOUGH those earliest locomotives (excepting the *Stars*) fell so far short of requirements, they were not, of course, all equally unreliable. Failures were, however, sufficiently serious and frequent to cause considerable anxiety to the directors, and so displeased were they with the general performance of the engines that they called upon Gooch, apart from his chief, Brunel, to report on each locomotive.

Gooch had hitherto done what he could to get the most out of a very indifferent lot of locomotives, and to keep them in some sort of working order, reporting upon their many and various deficiencies to Brunel. There is little doubt, therefore, that the request from the directors to report to them, independently of Brunel, put Gooch in a very difficult position. He had, however, no choice in the matter, and when his reports were duly made they generally condemned the construction of the engines.

Gooch says in his diary, on the subject of his report, that he received an angry letter from his chief, but adds that " Brunel was personally most kind and considerate, leaving him to deal with the engines as he thought fit," and (I like this touch) " his good sense told him that what I said was correct and his kind heart did me justice."

I think I ought to add that Gooch's report was principally concerned with the workmanship in the engines and contained little that could be construed as reflecting in any way upon Brunel.

The sequel to all this was that, shortly after, Gooch was asked to prepare designs for new locomotives, a large number of which were required. Here was undoubtedly Gooch's great opportunity, and he seems to have seized it with both hands. He records in his diary that he took great pains with his drawings which were for two classes of passenger engines ; one with single 7 ft. driving wheels and the other with single 6 ft. drivers, and cylinders of 15 ins. diameter and 18 ins. stroke, but with ample boiler power, of which some of those early troublesome engines had been remarkably deficient.

Gooch was fortunate in having as his chief draughtsman on this work Thomas R. Crampton, who afterwards made a name as a locomotive engineer and whose engines had a reputation on Continental railways. Lithographed detailed drawings of the new engines were distributed with printed specifications to each of the firms invited to tender, and sheet iron templates were prepared for the use of those builders whose contracts were accepted. Here, possibly, we have the first attempt at standardisation in locomotive construction, and interchangeability of parts.

Gooch was taking no chances with these engines and paid frequent visits to the contractors' works during the time that they were under construction.

In order that the experience with failing locomotives should not be repeated, Gooch was also careful to insert a clause in the contracts that the builders would be held liable for any breakage which might occur from faulty materials or bad workmanship " until each engine had performed a distance of 1,000 miles with proper loads," and a similar provision, I may add, has been made in such contracts up to the present time.

Contracts were then let for no fewer than 105 locomotives from various makers. Sixty-two of these engines were standard type passenger engines with 7 ft. driving wheels ; and 21 were passenger engines with 6 ft. driving wheels. It takes nothing from Gooch's reputation as a designer to

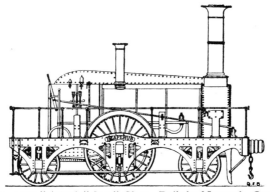

"Hesperus" (1841) " Sun " Class—Built by Nasmyth, Gaskell & Co., Manchester

say that these engines were direct derivatives of the *Stars* with improvements in detail based on experience for evidently Gooch had " hitched his wagon to a *Star*."

The remaining 22 locomotives consisted of goods engines, 18 of which had four-coupled 5 ft. driving wheels (2–4–0), and the other four six-coupled 5 ft. drivers (0–6–0). All the engines ordered were six-wheeled.

The first engine to be delivered was *Firefly* (March 12, 1840), which gave its name to the whole class of 7 ft. singles.

It is recorded that this engine ran from Paddington to Reading in 46½ minutes, with a load of three vehicles, a fortnight after delivery, while on the return journey a speed of 56 miles an hour was attained.

It was a sister engine *Ixion* which was used in 1845 when experiments were made by Gooch in preparing information for the Gauge Commission* as we shall see in a later talk. Another famous engine in this class was *Actaeon*,

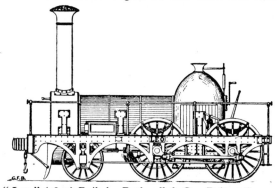

" Leo " (1841) Built by Rothwell & Co., Bolton, Lancs

which was used at the opening of the Bristol and Exeter Railway (May 1st, 1844). On that occasion Gooch himself drove the engine from London to Exeter and back over the G.W.R. and B. & E. Railways—a distance of 388 miles—and completed the return journey from Exeter to the platform at Paddington in 4 hours 40 minutes.

Engines of the " Firefly " class did good work for many years. Several of them were rebuilt between 1859 and 1865.

---

*See Track Topics.

They went out of service after 1870, as being too light for increased train loads, and owing to the conversion of sections of the line to narrow gauge.

The 21 engines with 6 ft. driving wheels were known as the " Sun " class after the first engine delivered, and were primarily intended for service between Swindon and Bristol, but were all converted to 2–2–2 saddle-tank engines, as were a few of the " Firefly " class. The last engine in

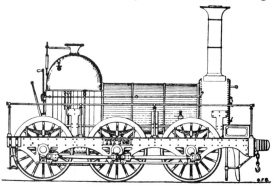

" Tityos " (1842) " Hercules " Class—Built by Nasmyth, Gaskell & Co., Manchester

this class to remain in service was *Gazelle*, which ceased work in 1879 (rebuilt 1864).

The four-coupled goods engines with 5 ft. driving wheels were known as the " Leo " class, and after a time they were found to be too light for the heavier loads of goods trains and were converted to 2–4–0 saddle-tank engines.

The six-coupled goods engines, known as the "Hercules" class, were an after-thought on the part of Gooch, who got the contractors to adapt four passenger engines for use as goods engines by fitting 5 ft. coupled wheels, altering the frames as required. They were the only six-coupled broad gauge engines ever built with the wheels inside the frames. These four engines all came into service in 1842 and ceased work in 1870–1. It was one of these engines *Sampson* which was used for the goods engine tests when preparing data for the Gauge Commissioners.

Here is a table giving some dimensions, etc., of the standard locomotives designed by Gooch.

Class	Wheel Arrangement	Cylinders Diam. Stroke	Diam. of Wheels		Boiler Press. lbs. per sq. in.*	Heating Surface Sq. ft.	Grate area Sq. ft.
			Driving	Carrying			
		ins.	ft. in.	ft. in.			
Firefly ..	2–2–2	15 × 18 (later enlarged to 16 × 20)	7 0	4 0	50	699	13.5
Sun ..	2–2–2	14 × 18 some 15 × 18	6 0	3 6	50	607.7	12.5
Leo ..	2–4–0	15 × 18	5 0 (coupled)	3 6	50	467	11.5
Hercules ..	0–6–0	15 × 18	5 . . 0 (coupled)	—	50	699	13.5

* Raised subsequently in many of the engines.

The last of the 7 ft. single-wheeler passenger engines was delivered in December, 1842, and after this date no further locomotives were built for the Great Western Railway until Swindon Works produced its first engine in 1846.

And the story of Swindon must be the subject of our next talk.

TALK NUMBER FIVE

SWINDON TAKES A HAND

Now we reach the point where Swindon comes into the story. By the end of July, 1840, the railway had been extended from the London end as far as Faringdon Road (now Uffington) and was nearing Swindon, whilst from the other end the section Bristol to Bath was fast approaching completion. Negotiations were also in hand for leasing the Bristol and Exeter Railway, and the line of railway between Swindon and Cheltenham. Furthermore, as delivery was soon to commence of the 105 odd engines of Gooch's design, which were being built by outside contractors, the question of providing a central repair depôt for the maintenance of locomotives had become a pressing one.

Gooch was called upon to investigate and report upon the most desirable place for such a depôt, and in selecting Swindon for the purpose he was influenced by the facts that it was both a convenient division of the line for engine working, and the junction for the Cheltenham Line.

Brunel and Gooch went together to look at the site and the Chief Engineer agreed with the choice of his Locomotive Superintendent. You get an idea of the locality before the coming of the railway and the effect of its advent in these extracts from an article " The Story of Swindon," written by Richard Jefferies (1848—1887), novelist and

Swirdon in 1849—Shewing Locomotive Works on left and Cottages etc., built for workmen on right

naturalist, who was born at Coate Farm, near Swindon. He says, writing in about 1880 :—

"There is but a faint, dim legend that the great Sweyn halted with his army on this hill—thence called Sweyn's dune, and so Swindon. There is a family here whose ancestry goes back to the times of the Vikings ; which was in honour when fair Rosamund bloomed at Wood-stock ; which fought in the great Civil War. Nothing further. The real history, written in iron and steel of the place began forty years ago only. Then a certain small party of gentlemen sat down to luncheon on the greensward which was then where the platform is now. The furze was in blossom around them ; the rabbits frisked in and out of their burrows ; two or three distant farm-houses, one or two cottages, these were all the signs of a human habitation, except a few cart-ruts indicating a track used for field purposes. There these gentlemen lunched, and one among them, ay, two among them, meditated great things, which the first planned, and the second lived to see realise the most sanguine anticipations. These two gentlemen were Isambard Brunel and Daniel Gooch . . . They decided that here should be their junction and their workshop . . . The green fields were covered with forges, the hedges disappeared to make way for cottages for the workmen. The workmen required food—tradesmen came and supplied that food—and Swindon rose as Chicago rose, as if by magic . . . In the Eastern tales of magicians one reads of a town being found one day where there was nothing but sand the day before. Here the fable is fact, and the potent magician is steam. Here is, perhaps, the greatest temple that has ever been built to that great god of our day . . . Where there was lately nothing but furze and rabbits there is now a busy human population. Why was it that for so many hundred of years the population of England remained nearly stationary? and why has it so marvellously increased in this last forty years? The history of this place seems to answer that interesting question. The increase is due to the facilities for communication which now exist, and to the numberless new employments in which that facility of communication took rise, and which it in turn adds to and fosters . . ."

Well, that tells you far better than I could what Gooch's selection of a site for the Great Western Railway Company's locomotive depôt had already meant to the little Wiltshire market town and countryside, more than half-a-century ago. You have seen for yourself what Swindon Works are like at present, covering 323 acres and employing

Interior of Engine House, Swindon, 1845

Swindon in 1847

about 12,000 workpeople.★   The locomotive section alone
has about 7,000 employees and repairs about 1,000 locomotives annually, and constructs approximately two new
engines per week.

But we must get back to the " eighteen-forties."   In
February, 1841, the directors authorised the establishment
of an engine depôt at Swindon, but in doing so no mention
was made of the building of new engines, and it is doubtful
if new construction was then even considered.   The
intention apparently was to provide a locomotive running
shed and repair works.   The running shed was opened the
following year with about 100 workmen, and the repair
workshop machinery was started in November, 1842, but
was not in regular operation until January of the following
year.

★See " Cheltenham Flyer."

Meanwhile, however, the great controversy between broad and narrow gauge had begun and was growing. There is little doubt that the speeds achieved by some of the G.W.R. broad gauge locomotives had the effect of exciting the envy of the narrow gauge railways and led to the improvement of their engines. This, not unnaturally, put the Great Western Railway directors upon their mettle, and early in the year 1846 we hear of Gooch being instructed to build " a colossal locomotive working with all speed."

You have heard the story of the " Battle of the Gauges " recently, and you know that a Royal Commission was appointed to enquire into and report upon the respective merits of the broad (7 ft.) gauge to which the Great Western Railway was constructed, and the narrow (4 ft. 8½ in.) gauge.*

The Gauge Commissioners sat for about five months and heard a mass of evidence from both sides. Gooch stated (as a witness) that in 1845, the express trains of the Great Western Railway were timed at an average over-all speed of 44 miles per hour, and a maximum speed of 60 miles per hour, between Twyford and Maidenhead, with loads of 70 or 80 tons behind the tender, and that he proposed to build engines of greater power.

Gooch, of course, championed the cause of the broad gauge before the Commissioners, and in that capacity he met some doughty opponents, among whom was Robert Stephenson. Their evidence turned on such technical subjects as comparative power and boiler evaporation, and it was after many weeks of argument that Brunel suggested

---

* See " Track Topics "

that, in order to test the accuracy of the opinions which had been expressed, trials of broad gauge and narrow gauge engines should be made under the eyes of the Commissioners. This suggestion hardly suited the narrow gauge party, and on various pleas they declined to commit themselves to long distance running, but it was ultimately agreed that trials should be made with train loads of 60, 70, and 80 tons between London and Didcot, a distance of 53 miles, and between York and Darlington, a distance of about 45 miles.

As I said in the last talk, the 7 ft. single-wheeler *Ixion* was selected for these tests, and the cylinders were enlarged to $15\frac{3}{4}$ ins. diameter and the boiler pressure raised to 75 lb. per square inch.

Three trips to Didcot and back were made. On the first down journey with 80 tons behind the tender, a maximum speed of 53 miles per hour was achieved, and 60 miles per hour on the return trip, which is very slightly down-grade. On the second trip when the load was reduced to 70 tons, practically similar speeds were obtained, while on the third trip (60 tons) the run from Paddington to Didcot was covered in 63 minutes 34 seconds, with an average speed of 50, and a maximum speed of 60 miles an hour ; and on the up journey the average speed was 53.9 and the maximum speed 61 miles an hour.

As regards the narrow gauge engine tests, which were made between York and Darlington, their performances were by no means equal to those of their rivals : the maximum speed achieved was $53\frac{3}{4}$ miles per hour, and this with a load of 50 tons only.

I am afraid that the methods adopted by both sides in these tests were not above question. It is stated that the feed water supplied to *Ixion* had been previously heated, but the narrow gauge people could evidently beat the broad gauge in devices of that kind for, not only was their engine tender filled with hot water before the start, but before the return trip, a powerful stationary engine was employed not only to provide hot water, but also to supply steam to the blower for creating a bright fire in the fire-box.

We must remember that one of the objects of the trials was to determine the thermal efficiencies of the respective engines, i.e., quantity of water evaporated per pound of fuel (coke) consumed during the runs, and it must be said that the dodges resorted to were more amusing than ingenuous. Apparently, however, no provisions had been laid down by the Gauge Commissioners as to the conditions regarding the feed water temperatures in these engine tests.

" Ixion " (" Firefly " Class)—Built in 1841 by Fenton, Murray & Jackson, Leeds

As I have already said, *Sampson*, one of the o–6–o engines of the " Hercules " class, was used for the goods engine trials, and on the run from Didcot to London, with a load of 400 tons behind the tender, *Sampson* achieved a speed of 25.7 miles an hour.

These trials completed the evidence taken by the Commissioners and they certainly proved the undoubted superiority of broad gauge engines. In fact the Gauge Commissioners report (1846) reads : –

" We feel it our duty to observe that the public are mainly indebted for the present rate of speed, and the increased accommodation of railway carriages to the genius of Mr. Brunel and the liberality of the Great Western Railway."

And in regard to the locomotive trials, the Commissioners reported :—

" We consider them (i.e. the trials) as confirming the statements and results given by Mr. Gooch, in his evidence, proving, as they do, that the broad gauge engines possess greater capabilities for speed with equal loads, and, generally speaking, of propelling greater loads with equal speed ; and moreover, that the working of such engines is economical where very high speeds are required, or where loads to be conveyed are such as to require the full power of the engine."

All that of course was a feather in the cap of Gooch, as well as being a tribute to Brunel.

As the Gauge Commissioners reported in favour of the narrow gauge in 1846 it is fairly obvious that in ordering the construction of their " colossal locomotive " in that same year, the directors were anticipating some renewal of the gauge war. The fate of the broad gauge, however, had already been sealed by the Commissioners' report although, as you know, broad gauge track did not finally disappear from the Great Western Railway for another 46 years, i.e., until May, 1892.

But we are still dealing with 1846. Gooch immediately set about the job of building that " colossal locomotive," and the directors' orders were fulfilled by the production of the appropriately named *Great Western*, the first locomotive to be completely constructed* at Swindon. The building of this engine was a wonderful achievement at that time, for design and construction together only occupied thirteen weeks. The staff worked day and night on the job and the engine was actually steamed on April 1st, 1846.

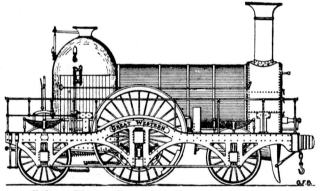

" Great Western " as originally constructed (2–2–2)

---

*" Premier," a goods engine (0–6–0) and one of a batch of six, was actually the first engine built at Swindon, but the boilers were supplied by outside contractors.

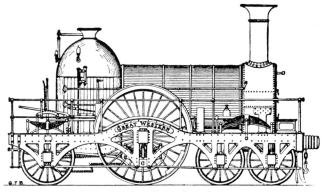
"Great Western" as altered to 4–2–2

Great Western was larger and more powerful than any locomotive extant, and was the prototype of a far-famed line of 8 ft. single-wheeled engines. The engine was originally of the 2–2–2 type, but the weight on the leading wheels was found to be too great and an extra pair of wheels was added. *Great Western* had a dome-top firebox, although this form was abandoned in succeeding engines in favour of the ordinary round top. In the latter form (4–2–2) twenty-four similar engines were built at Swindon and seven by an outside contractor.

These engines were fitted with " Gooch " link motion which had been produced in 1843* and took the place of the old " Gab " motion. The cylinders were 18 ins. diameter by 24 ins. stroke, the boiler pressure being 120 lb. A feature of these locomotives was that the tenders were provided with a seat at the back, facing the train, for the " travelling porter," whose duty it was to warn the driver

---

*Gooch's motion was fitted to most of the Swindon-built broad gauge engines and to the earlier narrow gauge engines.

"Centaur" ("Firefly" Class)—Built in 1841 by Nasmyth, Gaskell & Co., Manchester
(*Note the seat for Travelling Porter on the Tender*)

if anything happened to the train. Exponents of the narrow gauge facetiously referred to this porter as " the man in the iron coffin," and alleged that he was placed on the tender to give notice of the many dangers to which travellers on the broad gauge were exposed ! The official history of the Great Western Railway says that :—

" The business of the Travelling Porter is to ride on the seat placed for him on the tender, and to keep a steady and vigilant look-out along the side and top of the train, so that in case of accident to any of the carriages or of any signal from the guard, or any apparently sufficient cause that may come to his observation, he may at once communicate with the engineman, and if necessary stop the train."

All this was, of course, before the days of the communication cord or passengers' emergency signal and its intriguing £5 penalty for improper use.

Swindon's first locomotive was in many respects an epoch-making engine. It is recorded that as early as June, 1846, she did the $77\frac{1}{4}$ miles trip from Paddington to Swindon at an average speed of 59.4 miles an hour with a load of 100 tons behind the tender, and that was, indeed, good " going " for *Great Western* ninety years ago—don't you think ?

That brings our story to the point where Swindon is established as the birth-place of the Great Western Railway locomotives, and which seems a convenient close to this talk.

" Lord of the Isles "—Built at Swindon Works 1851.
Commenced work July 1852 and ceased work June 1884

TALK NUMBER SIX

GOOCH'S "EIGHT-FOOT-SINGLES" AND OTHERS.

WITH Swindon established as the birth-place of G.W.R. locomotives, perhaps it ought to be said at once that from that time forth (with certain exceptions which were more numerous prior to the narrow gauge era), practically the whole of the G.W.R. locomotive stock was built at Swindon or at the locomotive works later established at Wolverhampton.

Great Western, as I have already said, was a most successful locomotive, and a number of similar engines were put in hand, differing only from their prototype in that a round-top fire-box was substituted for the dome-top, or " Gothic," type.

Before these additional engines were ordered, however, *Great Western* was thoroughly put through her paces, and in the interim a batch of smaller passenger train engines with 7 ft. driving wheels, and known as the " Prince " class, after the first engine in the series, was built at Swindon. The last one (*Witch*) differed from the other five in that 7 ft. 6 ins. driving wheels were fitted.

The first of the " eight-foot-singles " to be built after *Great Western* was *Iron Duke* in April, 1847, and this engine gave its name to the whole class, which definitely made locomotive history. They had a great reputation for many years, in fact, they were larger and faster than any other engines previously constructed, and far ahead of any narrow-gauge locomotives of that time. They remained the standard engines for fast passenger train work on the Great Western Railway up to the time of the final gauge conversion in 1892.

Great Britain, one of the " Iron Duke " class, covered the 53 miles from Paddington to Didcot at an average speed of 67 miles an hour, and with another of the class a speed of 78.2 miles an hour was reached, probably for the first time by any railway locomotive, near Dauntsey on a falling gradient of 1–100.

There were six engines in the first lot built at Swindon. The driving wheels were flangeless,* and the carrying wheels were of 4 ft. 6 ins. diameter. As originally constructed, the boiler pressure was 100 lbs. per square inch, but this was later increased to 115 lbs. The tenders, which were on three axles with wheels of 4 ft. 6 ins. diameter, carried 1,800† gallons of water and 30 cwts. of coke.

The next batch of these engines, built at Swindon between 1848–1851, was known as the " Courier " class and differed only slightly in detail from the *Iron Dukes.* This series included *Lord of the Isles* the most famed as well as the fastest of Gooch's " broad-gaugers " and probably the speediest railway locomotive of its day. Built in 1851, *Lord of the Isles* was in regular service for 33 years without being re-boilered, and during that time ran 789,000 miles.

---

*Flanges appear to have been added to the driving wheels of these and others of the " Iron Duke " class about 1870-1.

†Tenders with a water capacity of 2,700 gallons were provided in 1864, for through running, London to Swindon.

If you compare this photograph of *Lord of the Isles* with that of *North Star* you will see how alike these two engines were except for the extra pair of front wheels.

During the period 1837—1851, however, locomotive power had been considerably increased, and *Lord of the Isles* with cylinders of 18 ins. diameter, and 24 ins. stroke had a boiler pressure of 140 lbs. to the square inch.

These engines were not only speedy and powerful, but of fine appearance with brass mounted boilers and wheel splashers. *Lord of the Isles* was in demand as an exhibit, and was on view at the Great Exhibition in Hyde Park in 1851, at the Edinburgh Exhibition in 1890, and at the Earls' Court Exhibition in 1897, although by that time the locomotive had been retired for 13 years.

This old favourite also went overseas and was shewn at the Chicago Exhibition in 1893. After such a glorious career it is unfortunate to have to record that she shared the fate of *North Star* and was broken up at Swindon in 1906.*

In the days of the old " eight-foot-singles," speed achievements were more of a novelty than they are now, and wonderful stories were told of what these old broad gauge locomotives had done and were doing, and some even more wonderful tales of what they *could* do. Some of those yarns were possibly of the " tall " variety, but one of an engine driver who offered to attempt the run Paddington to Bristol ($118\frac{1}{4}$ miles) in an hour was generally credited and regarded as well within the limits of possibility by many besides the driver who made the offer which, by the way,

---

* The valve gear of " Lord of the Isles " is preserved in Swindon College.

was coupled with a proviso that in the event of any cat-astrophe his family should be provided for !

The London to Bristol trip was actually covered by one of these engines with a load of 100 tons behind the tender in 2 hours 12 minutes, inclusive of nine and a half minutes spent in stoppages.

Trains hauled by these engines were booked in the time table to *leave* Didcot (53 miles from Paddington) 57 minutes after their departure from Paddington and repeatedly did the run in fifty minutes, and often in less.   And that in the " eighteen-forties " mark you !

∽   ∽   ∽   ∽

And now with your permission, having told the story of the earlier history of Great Western Railway locomotives, in some amount of detail, I should like to accelerate some-what as I am anxious, in due course, to devote as much time as possible to the examination of modern types of loco-motives.   Very well, then, without omitting anything that is really essential, we will now move a little faster.

Between the years 1846 and 1864, when Gooch retired from the position of Locomotive Superintendent of the Great Western Railway, he built at Swindon Works upwards of 120 broad gauge goods engines of the 0–6–0 type with 5 ft. wheels, besides sixteen of his famous " eight-foot singles."

Perhaps I ought to mention here a type of passenger saddle-tank engine designed by Gooch for the South Devon Railway and built at Swindon in 1849.   Only two were built, *Corsair* and *Brigand* and they were of 4–4–0 type, the coupled driving wheels being of 6 ft. diameter. *Corsair* was equipped with a sledge brake, fitted between the driving wheels, which when applied pressed on the rails, but this was found unsatisfactory (which is hardly surprising) and in *Brigand* brake blocks on the trailing wheels were substituted. Similar engines with 5 ft. 9 ins. driving

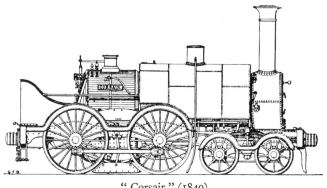

" Corsair " (1849)

wheels were built later (1854–5) and, with the two mentioned, became known as the " Bogie " class. In 1855 Gooch introduced a new type of 4–4–0 express passenger engine, of which ten were built by Robert Stephenson & Co., known as the " Waverleys " with names taken from Scott's novels. These engines had 7 ft. coupled driving wheels and cylinders 17 ins. by 24 ins. Owing to their long wheel base (17 ft. 11⅝ in.) they were not entirely suitable for express passenger working and were replaced by the " Victoria " class of 2–4–0 engines, which were built at Swindon from 1856 to 1864 with 6 ft. 6 ins. driving wheels, cylinders 16 ins. by 24 ins. and were named after

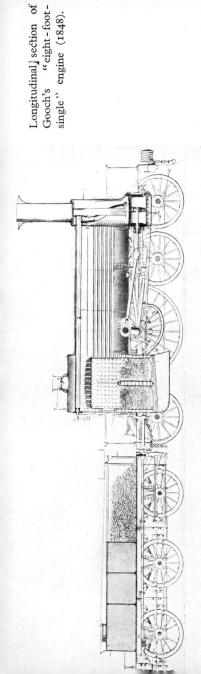

Longitudinal section of Gooch's "eight-foot-single" engine (1848).

"Waverley" (1855), built by Robert Stephenson & Co., Newcastle.

reigning monarchs of the period and (the last batch) after famous British engineers, beginning with Brunel.

Towards the close of Gooch's regime there were also constructed at Swindon ten Metropolitan side tank locomotives for working on the underground line between Bishop's Road (Paddington) and Farringdon Street Stations. These engines had four-coupled wheels of 6 ft. diameter with cylinders of 16 ins. diameter and 24 ins. stroke.

Gooch designed the first of the narrow gauge passenger locomotives for the Great Western Railway, and these (eight in number) were built in 1855 by Messrs. Beyer, Peacock & Co. of Manchester, and employed at first on the Birmingham and Chester services.

The first narrow gauge locomotive built at Swindon was a six-coupled goods tender engine. It was numbered " 57 " and, after rebuilding in 1870, actually survived until November, 1912, having completed 57 years of service and run well over a million miles.

We have now, I think, briefly covered the Gooch era, but perhaps it might be added that he designed engines for the Bristol and Exeter Railway, which were very similar to his *Iron Dukes*, but had 7 ft. 6 ins. driving wheels. Some of these engines survived until the B. & E. became part of the Great Western Railway.

After 27 years as its Locomotive Superintendent, Daniel Gooch left the Great Western Railway in 1864 to devote his energies to the great project of laying the Atlantic cable, having become a director of The Great Eastern Steamship Company four years earlier. As you know S.S. *The Great Eastern* was designed by his great friend Brunel, and Gooch had been a passenger on its first trip to America, in 1860. The first attempt to lay the cable was a failure, but that most difficult task was successfully accomplished in July, 1866, and, to mark its achievement, Gooch was created a baronet four months later.

Gooch returned to the Great Western Railway as its Chairman in 1865, at a time when the finances of the Company were in low water, but under his control (1865–1889) the Company was completely restored to prosperity. He was Member of Parliament for the Cricklade Division of Wiltshire from 1865 to 1885.

Gooch and Brunel were the two most historic figures in the early years of the Great Western Railway. Both were broad-gauge stalwarts, and together they securely laid the foundations of the G.W.R. tradition.

As Locomotive Superintendent Gooch designed engines which for power and speed were superior to any others of

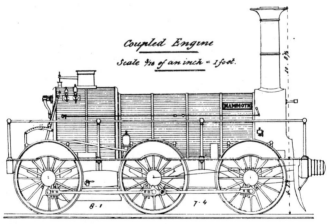

A drawing from Gooch's Sketch-book

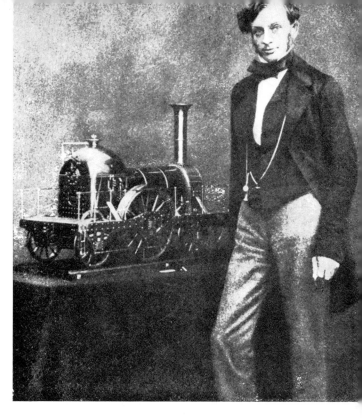

Daniel Gooch, in 1845

their time, and as Chairman he was responsible for seeing the Severn Tunnel scheme carried through, when the difficulties might have discouraged others less bold and confident.

As a financier he established the future of the Great Western Railway, and the man who did all this and more crowned all his achievements and earned the gratitude of his country by laying the first electric cable between this country and America. He died in 1889 and is buried in St. Andrew's Churchyard, Clewer, near Windsor.

His invaluable services to the Great Western Railway Company were recognised by the shareholders, who voted him a sum of money with which Gooch purchased

Sir Daniel Gooch

the beautiful centre-piece shewn in this photograph.

It is of solid silver and weighs nearly 500 ounces. The angles support statuettes of Brunel, Locke, and Stephenson, and the three panels at the base represent in bas-relief *The Great Eastern* steamship, *Windsor with Viaduct*, and the *Lord of the Isles* locomotive. The three panels contain the arms of Sir Daniel Gooch, Bart., The Great Western Railway, and an inscription, the whole being surmounted by a figure symbolical of science. The inscription is :—

The Silver Centre-piece

" Presented to Sir Daniel Gooch, Bart., M.P., by the Great Western Railway Company in recognition of the distinguished ability and success with which he has presided as Chairman over the administration of the Company's affairs, February 29th, 1872."

The centre-piece came into the possession of the G.W.R. Company a few years ago, and now stands in the Board Room at Paddington Station.

"Sultan," built in 1847. This engine was used by Frith as a model for his picture "The Railway Station."

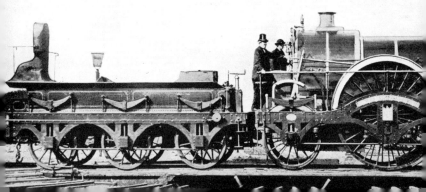

"Lord of the Isles" as decorated in connection with a Royal journey to Windsor.

SOME OF GOOCH'S FAMOUS "EIGHT-FOOT-SINGLES."

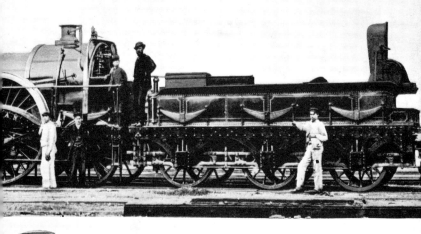

"Lightning," built in 1847 —ceased work in 1878. Ran 816,601 miles as originally constructed.

Standard Gauge (2–2–2)
" Queen," No. 55.
Built 1873.

Broad Gauge (2–4–0)
convertible No. 14.
Built in 1888.

TALK NUMBER SEVEN

1 8 6 4 — 1 9 0 2

MR. JOSEPH ARMSTRONG succeeded Mr. Gooch as Locomotive Superintendent of the Great Western Railway in 1864, and by that time a good deal of " mixed " gauge track existed ; that is, a third rail had been laid on much of the broad gauge track so that it could be used by vehicles of either broad or narrow gauge.

The demand for narrow gauge locomotives was increasing and, to meet it, standard 0–6–0 goods engines, " Metropolitan " passenger tank engines (with 6 ft. coupled driving and trailing wheels), and some 7 ft. single-wheeler engines were put in hand. Of the last named, a famous series of thirty was built, and the first engine produced (1866), and which gave its name to the class, was called *Sir Daniel* (No. 378) as a compliment to the first G.W.R. locomotive superintendent. These locomotives, which included the second *North Star* (No. 380) and *Morning Star* (No. 381), did the bulk of the narrow gauge express work for nearly three decades. As originally constructed they had 7 ft. driving wheels, domed boilers, and cylinders 17 ins. by 24 ins. stroke. After long and valuable service as passenger engines, twenty-one of them were converted in 1902 to 0–6–0 type goods engines with 5 ft. driving wheels.

A somewhat similar lot of engines was built at the G.W.R. Locomotive Works at Wolverhampton*, but these

---

*Wolverhampton was the chief centre for narrow gauge engine construction from 1859 to 1877.

had the Gooch type of sandwich framing and 6 ft. 6 ins. driving wheels. Eight such engines were constructed from 1872 to 1875, and about twenty years later they were rebuilt at Swindon as four-coupled engines.

In 1873 Swindon Works produced locomotive No. 55 appropriately named *Queen*, as for many years it was used for hauling royal trains. This engine was very similar to those of the " Sir Daniel " class, but was of rather heavier construction with cylinders of 18 ins. diameter. Twenty others were built in 1875, and these were used on express passenger train services, including that of $120\frac{1}{2}$ miles from Paddington to Worcester, which was scheduled to occupy 136 minutes only.

Another famous product of the Armstrong regime was a batch of six engines (439—444) built in 1868. These had coupled wheels of 6 ft. diameter (2–4–0) with cylinders 16 ins. by 24 ins. stroke and are of particular interest, not because they were the only locomotives of their type (2–4–0 tenders), but because they were the forerunners of the " Barnum " class from which in turn were descended the speedy *Cities*—of which you will hear more in due course.

It was during the last years of Mr. Armstrong's reign at Swindon that the Bristol and Exeter, South Devon, and Cornwall Railways became part of the Great Western Railway, and these amalgamations increased the Great Western Railway's stock of locomotives by nearly two hundred. Some of the engines thus acquired are worthy of notice.

The Bristol and Exeter Railway contributed some rather remarkable tank engines with monster flangeless driving

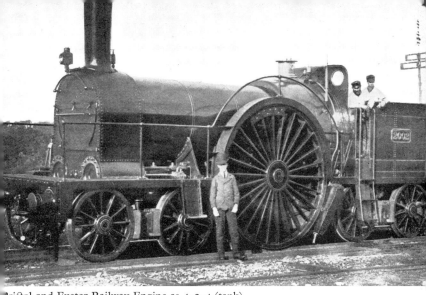

Bristol and Exeter Railway Engine as 4–2–4 (tank).

Same engine (G.W.R.) as converted to 4–2–2 (tender).

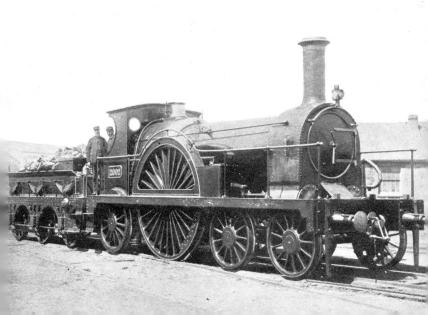

wheels of 8 ft. 10 ins. diameter, which were nearly level with the tops of the boilers. Built by Messrs. Rothwell and Company in 1868, they had a bogie at each end and were fitted with hand brakes operating on the trailing bogies only. Besides a back tank of 1,000 gallons capacity, they carried another four-hundred gallons of water in a tank between the frames. When taken over by the Great Western Railway, these curious 4–2–4T locomotives were altered to broad gauge tender engines, by removing the trailing bogie and substituting a pair of 4 ft. 6 ins. trailing wheels, thus converting them to 4–2–2's.

The South Devon Railway passenger locomotives were tank engines, principally built by the Avonside Company at Bristol, while a few had been originally purchased from the Great Western Railway. They were named, but not numbered, and here is a photograph of one (afterwards numbered 2132)—a four-coupled engine with 5 ft. 6 ins.

" Etna "—Built for the Carmarthen and Cardigan Railway in 1864.
Acquired by South Devon Railway 1868, and transferred to G.W.R. 1876.

South Devon Railway Engine No. 2132

driving wheels and a leading bogie (4–4–0T). The South Devon goods engines were six-coupled tanks (0–6–0T) with 4 ft. 6 ins. driving wheels.

Other railways absorbed during this period contributed a mixed lot of locomotives, a few of which were narrow gauge. Two which came from the Vale of Neath Railway were the first eight-wheeled coupled engines used in this country. In service they were found too heavy for the road, however, and ceased work in 1871.

If the period of Mr. Armstrong's control of locomotive design and production on the Great Western Railway was one of comparative conservatism with few striking innovations to record, it must be remembered that it was also the period when the broad gauge commenced to give place to the narrow or standard gauge and the policy was then one of gradual conversion, although the ultimate end of the broad gauge (which came in 1892) was not in sight.

Mr. William Dean, who at fifteen years of age had become a pupil of Mr. Armstrong when the latter was in charge of the G.W.R. Locomotive Works at Wolverhampton, and had risen to be Chief Assistant to Mr. Armstrong at Swindon Works in 1868, was appointed to succeed to the position of Locomotive Superintendent of the Great Western Railway on Mr. Armstrong's death nine years later (1877).

Mr. Dean made considerable additions to the G.W.R. locomotive stock in the quarter century during which he was Superintendent and this period coincided with increasing demands for engines for working the heavy merchandise and mineral traffic on the railway.

The first passenger engines built at Swindon by Mr. Dean were of the Gooch 2–2–2 type, being a batch of ten narrow gauge 7 ft. single-wheelers with cylinders 18 ins. by 24 ins. stroke, constructed in 1879. These were, perhaps, the speediest and best known locomotives of their time, being employed on express passenger trains and later on the " non-stop " runs London to Birmingham. One of these engines, No. 165, was actually in traffic working until 1915 and was the last survival of its type in service in this country.

Some at least of the later engines of this class (built about 1884–1886) had 7 ft. 8 ins. driving wheels and cylinders 18 ins. by 26 ins. In view of the pending abolition of the broad gauge these locomotives, with the older single-drivers, were chiefly responsible for maintaining the narrow gauge express passenger services until the final conversion of the broad to standard gauge in 1892.

In 1889 twenty narrow gauge four-coupled (2–4–0) engines, the *Barnums*, were built with 6 ft. 2½ ins. driving

Standard Gauge 7-ft. single-wheeler " Cobham " (1879)

wheels and cylinders 18 ins. by 24 ins. A similar number was constructed in 1892 in which the diameter of the driving wheels was increased to 6 ft. 8½ ins., and this latter dimension was destined to become a favourite for G.W.R. passenger engines for many years.

In 1891–2 a new class of 30 locomotives appeared, the first ten of which were built as broad-gauge convertibles and these were adapted to the narrow gauge with the final disappearance of the old 7 ft. track. They were 2–2–2's with 7 ft. 8 ins. driving wheels and cylinders 20 ins. by 24 ins. and with a boiler pressure of 160 lbs. per square

Broad Gauge 7 ft. 8 ins. single-wheeler " Bessemer " (1891)

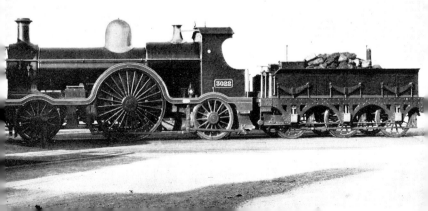

inch. Their weight (about 44 tons) proved too much for a single pair of leading wheels, and they were rebuilt in 1894 with leading bogies (4–2–2's). Thirty of these engines were produced in 1894 and twenty more in 1897. This fleet of single-wheelers, officially known as the " Achilles " class, after the first engine of the class (No. 3031), were generally referred to as " the thirties." They

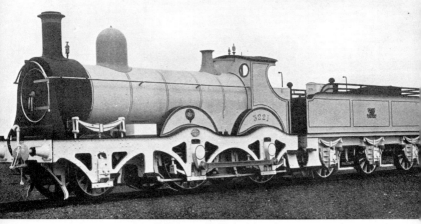

" Barnum " Class (2–4–0)

gave excellent service with light loads for many years. They included the third *North Star* of the Great Western Railway (No. 3072) and also *Duke of Connaught* (No. 3065) an engine which made history in May, 1904, in conjunction with *City of Truro* on a record breaking run with overseas mails from Plymouth to London. *Duke of Connaught* took the train over at Bristol from *City of Truro* and

"Achilles" (No. 3031)

brought it on to Paddington, actually covering the 118 miles 33 chains in less than 100 minutes without turning a hair, and then returned to Bristol two hours later with another mail train. Being short of adhesion, however, these engines were gradually broken up as train loads increased and heavier locomotives became necessary. The last of the class to survive was *Princess Helena* (No. 3074) which was scrapped in 1915.

When in May, 1892, the broad gauge finally disappeared, the stock of the broad gauge locomotives, which had been gradually reduced, consisted of 195 engines, of which 130 had been constructed as convertibles, so that the change-over actually only reduced the stock by 65 old-timers which

"Duke of Connaught" (No. 3065)

went to the scrap heap, excepting *North Star* and *Lord of the Isles* which, as you have been told, lived in retirement until 1906, when they too were broken up—although *North Star* was later reconstructed as already related.

" Tiny "

But no, I am wrong, the life of *one* old broad gauger was spared and that was *Tiny*, a queer little engine built for the South Devon Railway in 1869, taken over by the Great Western Railway in 1876, and used for some time on shunting work. She was later employed as a stationary

" Bulkeley " (4-2-2). The engine that hauled the last Broad Gauge train on the G.W.R. Built July, 1880, ceased work May, 1892.

engine for working pumps at Newton Abbot. Here is a photograph of *Tiny*, which has four coupled wheels (0–4–0) and a vertical tubeless boiler. She is now a " museum piece," and may be seen on the Down Platform at Newton Abbot Station. Although *Tiny* is the only survivor of the broad gauge era, she is, of course, in no way typical of broad gauge locomotives.

We now come to the year 1895, in which were built the first engines of the " Duke " class. They were of 4–4–0 type and had coupled driving wheels of 5 ft. 8 ins. diameter, being specially designed for working over the heavy gradients in the West of England, about which you already know something.*
You will remember too that on our trip to Swindon, which we made in order to return by *Cheltenham Flyer*, I explained that increased adhesion, that is increased grip of the wheels on the rails, was obtained by coupling the driving wheels together and how the smaller diameter wheels give greater tractive force.†
We shall touch on this again when considering just what the term " tractive force " means.

In the year 1895 the compulsory stop for refreshments at Swindon was (as you have been told) bought out at tremendous cost, and the regular running of through trains to the West of England was at last possible. Trains were soon running without intermediate stop from London to Bath, from London to Bristol, and from Newport to London ; and by 1896 through running from London to Exeter (193¾ miles) was introduced and was then the longest " non-stop " run in the world.

But let's get back to those first 4–4–0 type engines for they marked an important change in G.W.R. locomotive practice. As I said, they were designed for West of England traffic and they soon became known as the *Devonshires* although their official name was *Dukes*, after the first

---

*See " Track Topics."
†See " Cheltenham Flyer."

Broad Gauge Engines at Swindon awaiting conversion

engine of the class *Duke of Cornwall* (No. 3252) which, by the way, with others of the " Duke " class, is still in service.

The *Dukes* (or *Devonshires*) had 18 ins. by 26 ins. inside cylinders, domed boilers with a pressure of 160 lbs. per square inch, and round top fire boxes. The earlier engines were peculiar in that both bogie and tender wheels had

"Badminton" Class (4–4–0)

"Duke of Cornwall" (No. 3252

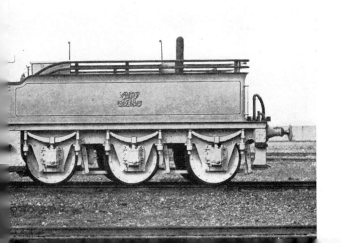

wooden centres, although the usual spoke pattern was reverted to in 1897. No fewer than forty engines of the " Duke " class were built in 1895 and 1896.

The year 1896 is important in G.W.R. locomotive history for it marks the birth of the 4–6–0 type. The first engine of the type (No. 36) was designed for heavy goods work, and had six-coupled driving wheels of 4 ft. $7\frac{1}{2}$ ins. diameter and cylinders 20 ins. by 24 ins., but others were of 2–6–0 type. Three years later a modification was introduced by building engines of this type with cylinders 19 ins by 28 ins. fitted with piston valves and, as they appeared about the time of the outbreak of the Boer War, they were known as the *Krügers*.

So successful were the *Dukes* that a similar kind of engine for long distance passenger train running on moderately graded tracks was designed with 6 ft. $8\frac{1}{2}$ ins. driving wheels and Belpaire type of fire-box. These were the *Badmintons* and you can see in this photograph how the general design of the locomotive had developed from the old *North Star* and was shaping towards the familiar lines of the engines of our own time. That big dome on the boiler was to disappear, but, disregarding it, you can see the transformation from 1836 to 1936 in progress.

Modifications in design of the *Dukes* produced the " Bulldog " class (1898), in which standard No. 2 boilers were fitted, and with this class the massive brass dome finally disappeared from G.W.R. passenger locomotives. Somewhat similarly from the *Badmintons* was developed the " Atbara " class (1900) and these were the first loco-motives to be built with the straight frame we know to-day ; thus we move another stage forward in design.

The *Atbaras* were also fitted with standard No. 2 boilers and in this class the pressure was raised to 180 lbs. per square inch.

The year 1900 saw the production of the *Aberdares* (2–6–0), so known because they were designed for work in South Wales. These engines were direct descendants of the *Krügers* but had a pair of leading wheels instead of a leading bogie. The coupled wheels were 4 ft. $7\frac{1}{2}$ ins. diameter, the cylinders 18 ins. by 26 ins., and the boiler pressure 2c0 lbs. per square inch. Since that time, a very large number of these useful engines have been built and they now carry standard No. 4 boilers.

That brings us to the end of our survey of locomotive development on the Great Western Railway during the years in which Mr. Armstrong and Mr. Dean were responsible for policy and production. Mr. Dean retired in May, 1902, but it should be added that the first 4–6–0 express passenger locomotive was actually completed at Swindon Works in February of that year. As, however, the development of the 4–6–0 passenger locomotive was left to Mr. Dean's successors, this is perhaps a convenient point at which to bring this seventh talk to an end.

" City of Truro " (No. 3440)

City of Truro made railway history in May, 1904, by achieving the highest speed attained by a railway train (102.3 miles an hour) when hauling an Ocean Mails Special from Plymouth to Bristol *en route* for London. This world's record stood unassailed for nearly thirty years and the achievement earned for *City of Truro* a place of honour in the Railway Museum at York, where it may be seen.

TALK NUMBER EIGHT

4 – 4 – 0 TO 4 – 6 – 0

M R. CHURCHWARD, who took office in place of Mr.
Dean in June, 1902, had served a pupilage with
Mr. John Wright, Locomotive Superintendent
of the old South Devon Railway, and entered
Great Western Railway service in 1877 in the Drawing
Office at Swindon. From that position he had risen by
stages to be Chief Assistant Locomotive, Carriage, and
Wagon Superintendent in September, 1897, so besides
being Mr. Dean's first assistant for nearly five years, Mr.
Churchward had been at Swindon throughout the entire
period of his predecessor's superintendency.

The opening years of the twentieth century saw the
adoption of a much more progressive policy by the Great
Western Railway than had obtained during the latter part
of the nineteenth, and Mr. Churchward's assumption of
office coincided with a call for heavier and more powerful
locomotives. Restaurant cars and corridor coaches had
considerably increased the weight of passenger trains, and
the use of the internal combustion engine in road motor
conveyance was already directing more attention to the
possibilities of higher general speeds and longer " non-
stop " runs on the railways.

The new Locomotive Superintendent was quite equal
to the demands of the times, as we shall soon see, and in
the year following his appointment, he produced the

famous " City " class engines of 4-4-0 type (which may be described as bigger *Atbaras*) with 6 ft. 8½ ins. coupled driving wheels, inside cylinders 18 ins. by 26 ins. and a boiler pressure of 195 lbs. per square inch. In the " City " class and its successors, Mr. Churchward not only dispensed with the dome on the boiler, but also with the perforated pipe for steam collection employed by some contemporary locomotove engineers. These changes were made possible by the additional steam space provided over the fire-box.

You have heard something of the speed achievements of the " City " class of engines. It was *City of Bath* (No. 3433) which drew the Royal train conveying the Prince and Princess of Wales (later King George V and Queen Mary) on a historic 246* miles " non-stop " journey from Paddington to Plymouth in 1903 at an overall average speed of 63.4 miles an hour, and actually covered the distance from London to Exeter (193¾ miles) at 67.3 miles an hour ! So impressed were those in authority at Paddington by this splendid performance that it led in the following year to the introduction into the timetable of the " Cornish Riviera Limited " train which ran " non-stop " from London to Plymouth and *vice versa*. The run from London to Plymouth was the longest regular train run without intermediate stop in the world when instituted, and for over twenty years afterwards.

Another of the " City " class, *City of Truro* (No. 3440) set up a wonderful record in 1904, not only for a railway train but for any form of mechanical locomotion, by attaining a speed of 102.3 miles an hour, when hauling an

---

*The route was then via Bristol.

"County of Middlesex" (No. 3473)

Ocean Mails special from Plymouth to Bristol *en route* for London. This world's record for a steam railway train stood unassailed for over thirty years. When retired from service in 1931 *City of Truro* was presented to the Railway Museum in York, where she can still be seen.

The "County" class, a new 4–4–0 type of passenger locomotive with outside cylinders 18 ins. by 30 ins. and 6 ft. 8½ ins. coupled driving wheels, appeared during 1904, and eventually forty engines of this class were built. The next year the "County Tanks" were produced, and these latter were a tank version (4–4–2T) of the "County" (tender) engines, with a trailing radial truck and the addition of side tanks and coal bunker. The "County" class engines were employed in main line express passenger services and the "County Tanks" on suburban passenger services for which their ability to run either end first (without turning at the end of the journey) made them particularly suitable.

We are not now adhering strictly to chronological order, as I want to finish for the present with the four-coupled

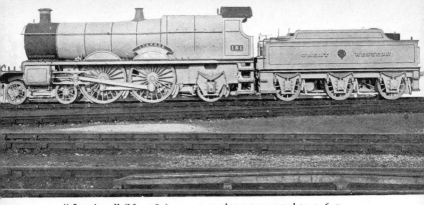

"Ivanhoe" (No. 181) as 4–4–2—later converted to 4–6–0

engines before coming to the 4–6–0 type. In 1905 some "Atlantic" (4–4–2) type passenger locomotives with outside cylinders 18 ins. by 30 ins. were built in which the boiler pressure was increased to 225 lbs. per square inch. These were named after old broad-gauge engines which bore the names of Sir Walter Scott's novels and became known as the "Waverley" class, the first produced being *Ivanhoe* (No. 181*). As, however, like all 4–4–2 passenger (tender) engines built at Swindon, they were eventually converted to 4–6–0 type, we need say no more about them at this stage.

In 1908 twenty more 4–4–0 engines were built for secondary passenger services, and being named after flowers (the first was *Auricula*, No. 4101), naturally became known as the "Flower" class. These engines had inside cylinders 18 ins. by 26 ins. driving wheels of 6 ft. 8½ ins. and a boiler pressure of 195 lbs. per square inch; in fact they were very similar to the "Atbara" and "City"

---

*Later renumbered 2981.

classes.   They were followed in 1909 by a batch of similar engines which, however, carried driving wheels of 5 ft. 8 ins. diameter.   This was the " Bird " class, the engines all being named after birds, the first to appear being *Blackbird* (No. 3441).   They were, in effect, modified *Dukes*.

That briefly brings us to the end of the story as far as four-coupled passenger locomotives are concerned.   It may at first sight appear somewhat strange that after single-wheelers had enjoyed such a long innings, the four-wheeled era for express passenger locomotives on the Great Western Railway should have been comparatively short. The explanation lies in the fact that train loads were becoming heavier and heavier, and longer runs at higher speeds were required.   In short, a fleet of locomotives with still greater power was being demanded for the principal main line express services, and the change to the 4–6–0 type was inevitable.

As you already know, the first six-coupled passenger locomotive (4–6–0) had been built at Swindon a few months prior to Mr. Churchward taking charge there. As a compliment to his predecessor the engine was named

" William Dean " (No. 100)

William Dean (No. 100*). This locomotive was unique when it appeared in 1902, as for the first time the cylinders were placed outside the frames, a reversal of previous practice, and adopted in order to accommodate the long stroke of the pistons (30 ins.) which, incidentally, was and still remains the longest stroke ever employed on the Great Western Railway. The cylinders were 18 ins. diameter, the coupled wheels 6 ft. 8½ ins. diameter, and the boiler pressure 200 lbs. per square inch.

In 1903 two more 4–6–0 engines (Nos. 98 and 171), somewhat similar to No. 100, were built. They were, however, fitted with larger cylinders having considerably enlarged steam and exhaust ports and carried larger boilers. In addition the boiler pressure of No. 171 (later named *Albion*),† was raised to 225 lbs. per square inch so that she could be tested in service with a French engine then on order, and of which more anon.

Now just a word about the coning of the boiler, before we proceed further, for this was an important development. By this provision the largest volume of water in the boiler came near the fire-box where the heat was greatest and you can well understand the advantage of that ; further, as the quantity of water at the other end of the boiler was comparatively small, any surging of the water from back to front (as on a descending gradient) could not materially affect the depth of water at the fire-box end, and, of course, you know what would happen if the crown of the copper fire-box was not covered with water.

---

*Later renumbered 2900.

†Named *The Pirate* (No. 2971) on conversion to 4–4–2, and renamed *Albion* after reconversion to 4–6–0 in 1907.

About this time much was being heard in technical circles about some famous du Bousquet-de-Glehn engines running on the Northern Railway of France and manufactured by the *Société Alsacienne de Constructions Mécaniques*. These were four-cylinder compound engines of

" Albion " (No. 171) as 4–4–2

4–4–2 type. The designers of these French engines claimed a considerably increased efficiency by applying the compounding principle to their locomotives, and in 1903 one of these engines, named *La France* (No. 102), was obtained by the Great Western Railway. This engine had a Belpaire firebox, two high pressure cylinders of 13.4 ins. diameter and two low pressure cylinders of 22.1 ins. diameter, the stroke being 25.2 ins. in both cases. It had divided drive (the inside cylinders driving the leading coupled axle and the outside cylinders driving the trailing coupled axle), separate valve gears for each pair of cylinders, and an intercepting valve which admitted live steam to the low pressure cylinders to augment the power required for starting and climbing. The coupled driving wheels were of 6 ft. 8 ins. diameter.

I said that in *Albion* (No. 171) the boiler pressure was increased to 225 lbs. per square inch, and that was done in order that it might approximate more closely to the boiler pressure of the French engine (227 lbs. per square inch) and, in addition, so that a fairer comparison could be made in actual work, *Albion* was, in December 1903, converted to 4–4–2 type.

You will be interested to know that *Albion*, with her two simple or single expansion cylinders, was able to compete very satisfactorily with *La France*. There was still some doubt as to the respective merits of four or six wheeled coupled engines, and this is instanced by the fact that in 1905 more engines of the " Albion " class were built, thirteen of these being constructed as 4–4–2's

" La France " (No. 102)

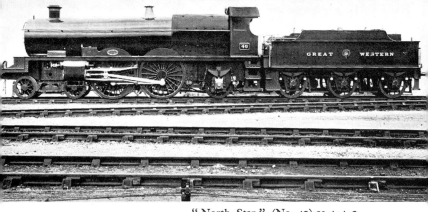

" North Star " (No. 40) as 4–4–2

and six as 4–6–0's, and all easily capable of conversion to either type according to results obtained in actual service. At the same time two more of the French four-cylinder compound engines were obtained. These were somewhat similar to *La France*, but were more powerful, having larger cylinders (H.P. 14.2 ins. and L.P. 23.6 ins.) and larger boilers. They were named *President* (No. 103) and *Alliance* (No. 104).

You will realise that, so far, the trials were between G.W.R. engines with two cylinders and French engines with four cylinders, consequently in order to make the comparison even more valuable, it was decided in 1906 to build a Swindon engine with four cylinders. This engine was built as a 4–4–2 (convertible to 4–6–0) and was named *North Star* (No. 40*). It was the fourth G.W.R. engine of that name and an epoch-making locomotive, for it was the first to be fitted with four high-pressure cylinders and, though the compounding principle of the French engines was not adopted, the divided drive was incorporated in its design.

---

*Later renumbered 4000.

North Star may be regarded as the progenitor of a famous class or rather classes, of G.W.R. four cylinder 4–6–0 express passenger engines to which type it was converted in 1909. Perhaps it is not putting it too high to say that the construction of *North Star* was the most important locomotive innovation during Mr. Churchward's regime.

In *North Star* the outside cylinders were placed outside the frames and over the rear wheels of the bogie, and the inside cylinders under and slightly in front of the smoke-box, an arrangement which has been followed ever since. The four cylinders were 14¼ ins. by 26 ins., the driving wheels 6 ft. 8½ ins., and the boiler pressure 225 lbs. per square inch, which gave a nominal tractive force of 25,085 lbs. The boiler was tapered throughout, but was in other respects similar to that of *Albion*.

The valve gear of *North Star* was of an unusual type. There were only two sets, fitted inside the frames, and the gear on each side of the engine received the principal part of its motion from the crosshead on the opposite side. The outside valves were operated by means of horizontal rocker arms from the inside gear.

North Star was unique in that it was not only the first four-cylinder locomotive ever built on the Great Western Railway, but also the only four-cylinder 4–4–2 engine on the Railway.

Well, you will want to know the result of the " 4–4–2 versus 4–6–0 " trials. The former engines had the great disadvantage of less adhesive weight than the 4–6–0's and this was brought out particularly on the steep gradients in the West of England, but in other respects also the

4–6–0 type proved to be the better, and it became the standard type for main line passenger working on the Great Western Railway.

There is a lot more to be said about that fine engineering product, the G.W.R. four-cylinder 4–6–0 type locomotive, but having got it established we will conclude this talk, which roughly covers the first five years of Mr. Churchward's superintendency, which, I think you will agree, was a most eventful one in G.W.R. locomotive history.

"Lady of
the Lake"
(No. 2902)

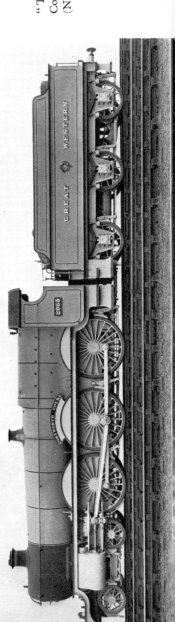

"Tortworth
Court"
(No. 2955)

TALK NUMBER NINE

4-6-0's ESTABLISHED —
SUPERHEATING, ETC.

A s we have seen, the wheel arrangement (4–6–0) for express passenger locomotives was settled after the trials with the French engines, and although the engines of the four-coupled " Flower " class were built subsequently, they were for subsidiary passenger services. The " Waverley " class, built as 4–4–2's in 1905, were later converted to 4–6–0's.

In 1906–7 the " Lady " and " Saint " classes of two-cylinder 4–6–0 engines had been brought out and these were very similar to " Albion " except that, in the " Saint " class, the cylinder diameter was increased to $18\frac{1}{8}$ ins.   The next batch, named the *Courts*, differed but slightly from their predecessors, the cylinders were $18\frac{1}{2}$ ins. by 30 ins., and the boiler pressure of 225 lbs. to the square inch was retained.   In the *Courts*, however, the framing was improved by being dropped at the ends, as you see in this photograph, and from which you will also observe that the familiar outline of modern G.W.R. express locomotives had almost completely developed.

In 1907 and 1908 twenty more four-cylinder passenger engines of 4–6–0 type were built and were named *Stars* and *Knights*. These engines together with the *Kings* (after-wards renamed *Monarchs*, and not the *Kings* we know to-day), *Princes and Princesses*, were all of the " Star " class and hauled the long distance express passenger trains for many years. Several of these engines are still doing useful work. They had four cylinders $14\frac{1}{4}$ ins. by 26 ins., driving wheels of 6 ft. $8\frac{1}{2}$ ins. diameter, and with a boiler pressure of 225 lbs per square inch. developed a tractive effort of 25,085 lbs. The weight of the engines ready for the road was 75 tons 12 cwt., while the tenders of 3,500 gallons water capacity weighed 40 tons full, giving a total weight of engine and tender (full) of 115 tons 12 cwts.

The cranks of the four-cylinder engines quartered the circle, the inner and outer cranks on the same side being at an angle of 180 degrees.

I ought to add that one engine, *Prince of Wales* (No. 4041), built in 1913, was experimentally fitted with 15 ins. cylinders, and as a result during the next year fifteen more (*Princesses*) were built with the larger cylinders, thereby increasing the tractive effort to 27,800 lbs.

In following the development of the famous " Star " class of four-cylinder 4–6–0 locomotives, we have had to depart considerably from date order, and one event which has been omitted is the production of the first and only

" Evening Star " (No. 4002)

"Prince of Wales" (No. 4041)

locomotive of "Pacific" type (4–6–2) on the Great Western Railway. *The Great Bear* (No. 111) was completed in June, 1908, and was a larger edition of the "Star" class —the cylinders, motion, expansion gear, axles and bogies being similar.

Owing to the size and weight of *The Great Bear*, which was 71 ft. $2\frac{1}{2}$ ins. in length (engine and tender) and turned the scale in working order at 142 tons 15 cwts., its use was much restricted. We shall have something more to say about this engine a little later on.

I have said that *The Great Bear* was the only locomotive of "Pacific" class on the Great Western Railway; it was also the only representative of its class in this country for fourteen years.

So far, our talk about Mr. Churchward's regime has been concerned with express passenger engines, but whilst perhaps development in this direction is more spectacular, it represents only one phase of locomotive progress made from 1902 to 1921.

In 1903 the first 2–8–0 type engine in this country was produced at Swindon. It was designed for hauling heavy

"The Great Bear" (No. 111) as a Pacific type (4-6-2), later converted to "Castle" Class (4-6-0) and re-named "Viscount Churchill."

mineral trains, and between 1905 and 1907 thirty were built, having outside cylinders 18 ins. or $18\frac{3}{8}$ ins. and 200 lbs. boiler pressure. These engines comprise the " 2800 " class, carrying tapered boilers with Belpaire fire-boxes. Fifty-odd engines of this class built between 1911 and 1919 had cylinders of $18\frac{1}{2}$ ins. diameter and boilers similar to the " Saint " class of 4-6-0 passenger engines, with 225 lbs. boiler pressure, and eventually all engines of the class were similarly equipped.

The first of the 2-6-2T or " Prairie " type engines (" 5100 " class) appeared about this time and subsequently 160 of this class of engine were constructed. They have cylinders 18 ins. by 30 ins., coupled wheels of 5 ft. 8 ins. diameter, and boiler pressures of 200 lbs. per square inch. The tanks were originally of 1,380 gallons water capacity, but have since been increased to 2,000 gallons.

The " 4200 " class, 2-8-0T goods engines appeared in 1910 and were the first 2-8-0 tank engines to be built in this country, in which they are unique. They have coupled driving wheels of 4 ft. $7\frac{1}{2}$ ins. diameter, outside cylinders 19 ins. by 30 ins., a boiler pressure of 200 lbs., and tanks of 1,800 gallons capacity.

A particularly useful type of engine for mixed traffic working was first built in 1911. This was the 2-6-0 type, known as the " 4300 " class. These engines have outside cylinders $18\frac{1}{2}$ ins. by 30 ins., 5 ft. 8 ins. driving wheels, and a boiler pressure of 195 lbs. They are, in fact, ' tender ' versions of the 2-6-2T type with which all parts are interchangeable. So successful have these engines been since their introduction that to-day the stock is round about 340.

"2800" Class (2–8–0)

Mr. Churchward's era covered the period of the Great War, and there was naturally a cessation of locomotive development until after the end of hostilities. Although standard type engines were produced, the activities of the Swindon Works were largely devoted to the supplying of war material.

Six months after the Armistice, a new type of locomotive was produced at Swindon. This was a 2–8–0 engine, of which seven were built ("4700" class), being designed for long distance goods trains and heavy mixed traffic—a development of the 2–6–0, but with more adhesive weight.

ဢ   ဢ   ဢ   ဢ

This talk and the preceding one briefly cover locomotive progress on the Great Western Railway during Mr. Churchward's nineteen years' regime, but I must not omit to mention that in 1904 the first steam rail car for light passenger traffic was built at Swindon. Some of these are 70 feet in length, and can be used with or without trailers. They can be driven from the engine end or from the other end of the trailer when employed in " shuttle " services, as they so often are. These rail motors are gradually being superseded by 0–4–2T and 0–6–0T engines, used with trailers, when they are known as " auto-engine " sets.

Mr. Churchward's period of office was one of great development. He was responsible for many innovations and improvements in locomotive construction and did much to build up what I have already referred to as the G.W.R. tradition.

He was responsible for introducing standardisation, not only in locomotive types but also in their parts, such as boilers, bogies, cylinders, motion, expansion gear, etc., and what this meant in the way of economy may be judged by the case of the boilers. Prior to standardisation, each class of locomotive and in some cases, each locomotive, had a different type of boiler, and when the boiler went in for repairs, or was out of service for any reason, the locomotive was necessarily idle. Under Mr. Churchward's scheme standard types of boilers were available for several classes of locomotives and if boiler repairs were in any

" 4200 " Class (2–8–0T)

way protracted, a new, or repaired boiler was fitted forthwith and the locomotive was available for service after only a minimum of time in which to effect the exchange.

Two other items for which Mr. Churchward was responsible in introducing in Great Western practice are superheating and " top-feed " to the boilers. In the latter arrangement the feed water from the injectors enters the boiler through a chamber incorporated in the safety-valve casting and percolates into the boiler barrel over a series of perforated steel trays, thereby tending to assist in the important problem of maintaining correct circulation of the water system. With regard to superheating, as early as 1906, Mr. Churchward had experimented with the " Schmidt " apparatus and soon after he fitted three of the *Stars* with superheaters. *Western Star* (No. 4010) was fitted with the Cole apparatus in 1907, *Knight of the Garter* (No. 4011) with what became known as " Swindon No. 1 " superheater in 1908, and *King Edward*★ (No. 4021) with " Swindon No. 3 " superheater. The last named apparatus (an improvement on " Swindon No. 1 ") is now the G.W.R. standard superheater.

This seems as good a place as any in which to say a few words about superheating which, simply stated, is adding heat to steam after it has ceased to be in contact with water, above its generation temperature.

The superheater elements are located in rows of larger tubes above the ordinary boiler flue tubes ; a unit consisting of six tubes forming three distinct loops, both ends

---

★Later renamed *British Monarch*.

of which are in a hollow horse-shoe shaped member that is bolted to the " header," which is a large iron casting, resting on brackets across the smoke-box, in front of the large superheater tubes. Contained in this casting are two chambers, one for saturated steam, and one for super-heated steam. Thus the header receives saturated steam from the boiler via the regulator box, directs it through the elements, and thence in its superheated state through copper pipes to the steam chests of the cylinders.

But here is a diagram of the most modern type of " Swindon " superheater. Let's look carefully at it and see if we can understand its construction and how it works. . . . As you see, it consists of the main header " A " which stretches across the smoke-box, a number of U-shaped junction headers " B " extending like fingers at the top and bottom of the main header to which they are bolted, and a series of superheater tubes " C " which are expanded into the junction header and terminate in bends " D."

The superheater tubes are stiffened by perforated plate supports " E " through which they pass and project into two rows of large flues " F " in the boiler. These supports serve the additional purposes of disturbing and churning up the heated gases as they pass through the flues.

The smoke-box portion of the superheater is enclosed by the casing " G," the front of which is hinged to give access to the apparatus, the bottom being left open for the passage of the flue gases under the deflector plate " H " to the chimney.

Saturated steam passes from the boiler through the regulator " K " and the steam pipes " L " to the top chamber of the main header " A " and thence to one finger

of the junction header " B " through the small tubes " C "
and bends " D " to the other finger, and from there to the
bottom chamber of the header and via the steam pipes
" M " to the steam chest and on to the cylinders. The
course of the steam is indicated by arrows in the diagram.

I hope this is clear, and now you will probably ask what
advantages are gained by superheating. Well they include
(1) the conversion into steam of water particles carried over
from the boiler (2) an increase in the volume of steam
produced by the boiler (3) the reduction of condensation
of the steam in the engine cylinders. All these factors
greatly improve the efficiency of the locomotive, as, by
increasing its temperature more use can be made of the steam
in the cylinders, the effect of which is to reduce the consumption of coal for a given amount of work which the
engine performs.

Perhaps I need say no more on the subject except that
superheating is so valuable a provision that all G.W.R.
locomotives, with the exception of shunting engines, are
now equipped with superheating apparatus.

We have now reached a point in the history of Great
Western Railway locomotives where we might well take
stock of what had then been accomplished.

As we have seen under Mr. Gooch, the boiler pressure
per square inch was increased from 50 to 120 lbs., while
in Mr. Armstrong's time it advanced to 160 lbs., and in
Mr. Dean's time to 200 lbs.; reaching as high as 225 lbs.
under Mr. Churchward. This was a good record, and
with the introduction of top-feed to boilers, superheating,
standardisation and interchangeability of parts, water-
troughs in the track, and water softening plants which

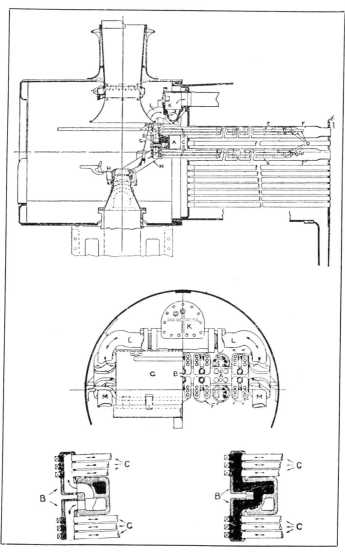

Diagram of G.W.R. Standard Superheater

reduced the attention necessary to boilers—all these in Mr. Churchward's time—resulted in putting Great Western Railway locomotives well in the forefront for speed, power, and reliability.

Before concluding this talk I ought to add that in the year 1916 the title of Locomotive, Carriage and Wagon Superintendent was changed to that of Chief Mechanical Engineer.

Mr. Churchward retired at the end of the year 1921 after nineteen years of valuable and progressive work as the directing force in G.W.R. locomotive design and construction.

The accompanying statement gives the years in which the first engines of various types were built, with some salient particulars, and summarises locomotive development during Mr. Churchward's period of office.

LOCOMOTIVE TYPES INTRODUCED 1902-1919

P—Passenger. **G**—Goods. **M**—Mixed Traffic. **B**—Branch. *See last column.*

Date	CLASS. Name	CLASS. No.	Type	CYLINDERS. No.	CYLINDERS. Diam. and Stroke	*Boiler Pres. lbs. per sq. in.*	*Diam. of Coupled Wheels.*	
					ins.		ft. ins.	
1902	*William Dean* ..	2900	4-6-0	2 outs.	18 × 30	200	6 8	**P**
1903		2611	2-6-0	2 ins.	18 × 26	200	4 7½	**G**
1903		3100	2-6T-2	2 outs.	18 × 30	195	5 8½	**M**
1903	*City of Bath* ..	3710	4-4-0	2 ins.	18 × 26	195	6 8½	**P**
1903	*Ernest Cunard* ..	2998	4-6-0	2 outs.	18 × 30	200	6 8½	**P**
1903	*La France* .. (purchased)	102	4-4-2	4 { 2 hp. 2 lp. comp'nd	13⅜ × 25 3/16 22 1/16 × 25 3/16	227	6 8	**P**
1903	*Albion* ..	171	4-6-0	2 outs.	18 × 30	200	6 8½	**P**
1904	*Albion* converted to	2971	4-4-2	2 outs.	18 × 30	200	6 8½	**P**
1904	*County of Middx.*	3800	4-4-0	2 outs.	18 × 30	300	6 8½	**P**
1904		4400	2-6T-2	2 outs.	16½ × 24	165	4 1½	**G**
1905	*Alliance* and *President* (purchased)	103 & 104	4-4-2	4 { 2 h.p. 2 l.p. comp'nd	14 3/16 × 25 3/16 23⅝ × 25 3/16	227	6 8	**P**
1905		2801	2-8-0	2 outs.	18 × 30	200	4 7½	**G**
1905	*County Tank* ..	2221	4-4T-2	2 outs.	18 × 30	195	6 8½	**P**
1905	*Ivanhoe*	181	4-4-2	2 outs.	18 × 30	225	6 8½	**P**
1906	*Krugers* converted		2-6-0	2 ins.	18 × 26	200	4 7½	**G**
1906	*Lady Superior*	2901	4-6-0	2 outs.	18 × 30	225	6 8½	**P**
1906	*North Star* ..	40	4-4-2	4	14 × 26	225	6 8½	**P**
1906		4500	2-6T-2	2 outs.	17 × 24	180	4 7½	**G**
1907		2821	2-8-0	2 outs.	18⅜ × 30	225	4 7½	**G**
1907	*Albion* reconverted	2971	4-6-0	2 outs.	18 × 30	225	6 8½	**P**
1907	*Dog Star* ..	4001	4-6-0	4	14¼ × 26	225	6 8½	**P**
1907	25—'s converted to	3901	2-6T-2	2 ins.	17½ × 24	180	5 2	**M**
1907	*Prairie Tank* ..	3151	2-6T-2	2 outs.	18½ × 30	200	5 8	**M**
1908	*The Great Bear* ..	111	4-6-2	4	15 × 26	225	6 8½	**P**
1908	*Auricula* (Flowers)	4101	4-4-0	2 ins.	18 × 26	195	6 8½	**P**
1909	*Blackbird* ..	3441	4-4-0	2 ins.	18 × 26	195	5 8	**P**
1909	*North Star* converted	4000	4-6-0	4	14¼ × 26	225	6 8½	**P**
1910	*Consolidation Tank*	4201	2-8T-0	2 outs.	18½ × 30	200	4 7½	**G**
1911		2831	2-8-0	2 outs.	18½ × 30	225	4 7½	**G**
1911		4301	2-6-0	2 outs.	18½ × 30	200	5 8	**M**
1912	*Ivanhoe* converted to	2981	4-6-0	2 outs.	18 × 30	225	6 8½	**P**
1913		4530	2-6T-2	2 outs.	17 × 24	200	4 7½	**G**
1913		4600	4-4T-2	2 outs.	17 × 24	200	5 8	**B**
1913	*Prince of Wales* ..	4041	4-6-0	4	15 × 26	225	6 8½	**P**
1919		4700	2-8-0	2 outs.	19 × 30	225	5 8	**M**

"Cheltenham Flyer" at speed

—

Drawn by Engine "Barbury Castle" (No. 5043)

TALK NUMBER TEN

"CASTLES," "HALLS," AND OTHERS

MR. CHURCHWARD was succeeded by Mr. C. B. Collett, who had entered Great Western Railway service in the Drawing Office at Swindon in 1893, and had been appointed to the position of Deputy Chief Mechanical Engineer in 1919.

Mr. Collett took office in January, 1922. In the year of his appointment the " Abbeys," the last batch of four-cylinder 4–6–0 " Stars " appeared, and with their construction balanced inside cranks were adopted, which since that time have been standard practice for all G.W.R. four-cylinder engines.

Mr. Collett's appointment synchronized with the operation of the Railways' Act of 1921 under which the whole of the railways of the country, with certain exceptions, were divided into the four big groups which we know to-day.

Under this Act the Great Western Railway absorbed a number of smaller undertakings including the Cambrian, Taff Vale, Barry, and other Railways, and as a result a miscellaneous stock of engines of various types was acquired. As these engines have come into the shops they have been brought into line with G.W.R. standards as far as possible, and while some are still in service, many have now found their way to the scrap heap.

Among the railways taken over under the Act was the Vale of Rheidol Line (from Aberystwyth to Devil's Bridge) which has a gauge of 1 ft. 11½ ins. only, and new locomotives for this railway were built at Swindon in 1923.

The year 1923 saw the production of the prototype of the famous " Castle " class, *Caerphilly Castle* (No. 4073) which was then the most powerful passenger train engine in Great Britain.

The *Castles*, which are four-cylinder 4–6–0 type engines, are a development of the " Star " class, but possess several distinctive departures. They have larger cylinders (16 ins. by 26 ins.), and to supply them with steam a new boiler was designed with a pressure of 225 lbs. per square inch, in which the dimensions were increased, the barrel being 5 ft. 1$\frac{15}{16}$ ins. in diameter at the front and 5 ft. 9 ins. at the throat plate ; the length remaining at 14 ft. 10 ins., which is that of the No. 1 standard boiler.

The inside cylinders are supplied with steam through passages in the saddle supporting the smoke-box, the steam pipes for the outside cylinders being brought through the side of the smoke-box and connected direct to the steam chests.

The provision of these larger cylinders brought the tractive effort up to 31,625 lbs. (at 85 per cent. boiler pressure) compared with 27,800 lbs. of the former four-cylinder class.

The *Castles* have longer frames than former engines of their type, and advantage has been taken of this to provide a more roomy cab. None of the fittings in the cab projects beyond the regulator handle, so that greatly increased space is available for the engine crew. Additional windows were provided in the cab and the roof was considerably extended. A new feature of the " Castle " class

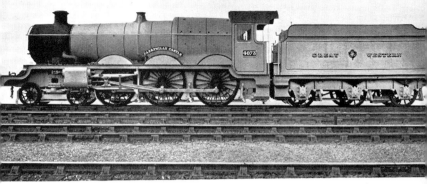

"Caerphilly Castle" (No. 4073)

of locomotives was the provision of tip-up seats for both driver and fireman.

Here is a photograph of a "Castle" class locomotive and also a diagram giving the salient dimensions. You will observe that the weight of engine and tender in working order is approximately 120 tons.

Caerphilly Castle was exhibited at the British Empire Exhibition in 1924, and was on view to the public in the Palace of Engineering where it was admired by vast crowds. From the opening of the exhibition in April to its close in October there was almost a continuous stream of visitors, including a big proportion of "boys of all ages" waiting to go into the cab and inspect Britain's most powerful passenger locomotive.

The *Castles* have proved themselves in service among the speediest locomotives in the world, and a "Castle" class engine regularly hauls the famous *Cheltenham Flyer* express of which you already know a good deal, including the facts that it was the first steam train regularly booked at an average speed of over 70 miles an hour, and that it

DIAGRAM OF G.W.R. FOUR-CYLINDER (4-6-0) "CASTLE" CLASS LOCOMOTIVE

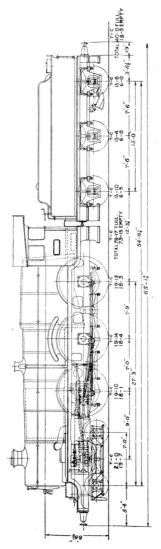

DESCRIPTION

CYLINDERS (FOUR)—Dia., 16"; Stroke, 26"; Steam ports, 25" by 1¼"; Exhaust, 25" by 3".

BOILER—Barrel, 14' 10"; Dia. Outs. 5' 9" and 5' 1½".

FIREBOX—Outside 10' 0" by 6' 4' 0"; Inside, 9' 2 5/16" by 5' 0 3/8"; Height, 6 8⅞" and 5' 3⅞".

TUBES
Superheater tubes, No. 84, Dia., 1"; length, 15' 3⅞".
Fire tubes, No. 201, Dia., 2"; No. 14, Dia., 5⅞" length, 15' 2 7/16".

HEATING SURFACE
Superheater tubes 262.62 sq. ft. } Total
Fire tubes .. 1,885.62 sq. ft. } 2312.0
Fireboxes .. 163.76 sq. ft. } sq. ft.

AREA OF FIREGRATE—30.28 sq. ft.

WHEELS—Bogie, 3' 2"; Coupled, 6' 8½".

WATER CAPACITY OF TENDER—3,500 gallons.

WORKING PRESSURE—225 lb. sq. in.

TRACTIVE EFFORT—31,625 lb.

daily performs the fastest " start to stop " run in the British Isles by covering, at an average speed of 71.3 miles an hour, the $77\frac{1}{4}$ miles from Swindon to Paddington.

Tregenna Castle (No. 5006), you will remember, made a marvellous run with *Cheltenham Flyer* on June 6th, 1932, when the distance from Swindon to Paddington was covered in 56 minutes 47 seconds, and 39 miles of this at an average speed of 90 miles an hour ! Yes, these *Castles* are the greyhounds of the Great Western Railway service, and when in June, 1935, the *S.S. Normandie* broke the record for the Atlantic crossing, and the Great Western Railway took up the race at Plymouth, overseas passengers were conveyed by special train headed by *Dynevor Castle* (No. 4094) from Plymouth Docks to Paddington—a distance of 226 miles 77 chains—in three hours thirty-eight minutes !

It was a " Castle " class locomotive, *Windsor Castle* (No. 4082), which had the unique distinction of being driven by the late King George V. Accompanied by Queen Mary he paid a visit to Swindon Works some years ago, and upon conclusion of the royal tour, took the driver's place at the controls and, with his Queen Consort beside him on the footplate, drove the engine of the royal train from the Works to Swindon Station, a distance of nearly a mile, to the delight of thousands of cheering workers assembled along the track. This locomotive was also selected to convey the body of our late Sovereign and the Royal Funeral party from Paddington to Windsor on January 28th, 1936.

Thirty " Castle " class engines are being built in this year's locomotive programme at Swindon Works, and these will bring the number of these most useful and speedy engines up to 101, and included in this figure is *Viscount Churchill* (No. 111) formerly *The Great Bear* which, in 1924, was reconstructed as a " Castle " class engine. The figure also includes four of the older four-cylinder engines —*Knight of the Golden Fleece* (No. 4016), *Queen Alexandra* (No. 4032), *Queen Philippa* (No. 4037) and *North Star* (No. 4000) which have been converted to " Castle " class.

Up to the year 1925, the semi-fast passenger and fast goods trains had been worked principally by engines of the " 4300 " class, but the need for a more powerful engine on these classes of work was becoming evident. The traffic demands were therefore fulfilled by the construction of the 4–6–0 " Hall " class engines, which among other features, have two outside cylinders, driving wheels of 6 ft. diameter, " Castle " class cabs, and a tractive effort of 27,275 lbs. These engines have been very successful in service, and no fewer than eighty were constructed between 1928 and 1930.

A " Castle " in the air

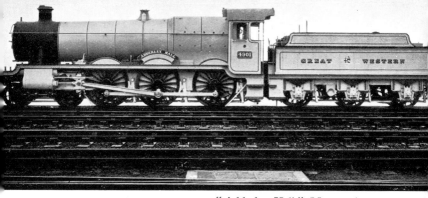

"Adderley Hall" (No. 4901)

By the end of 1935 the fleet of "Hall" class engines had been increased to 150, and the 1936 programme provided for the construction of a further batch of ten.

One hundred new engines of 4–6–0 type, very similar to the "Hall" class, but with 5 ft. 8 ins. diameter driving wheels, are to be built. They are designed for dealing more expeditiously with fast freight services, such as the broccoli trains from Cornwall, the fruit trains from Worcestershire, and heavy excursion trains.

Some of these engines will form the new "Grange" class, the first engine in the class being named *Arlington Grange* (No. 6800). Cylinders of an improved design are being fitted, but the bogies are of standard pattern. The larger boiler and increased boiler pressure will give a greater tractive effort (28,875 lbs.) and enable them to maintain high speeds over much greater distances than the "4300" class of 2–6–0 engines which they will supersede.

From 1923 onwards new classes of goods, mixed traffic, and shunting engines, including auto-engines of 0–6–0T and 0–4–2T types (which with the special passenger stock provided, do the work hitherto carried out by rail motors) were produced, and these are summarized in the accompanying table which gives the year of introduction of new types, together with wheel arrangements, cylinder dimensions, boiler pressures, and diameter of coupled wheels.

LOCOMOTIVE TYPES INTRODUCED 1922-1936.

P—Passenger. G—Goods. M—Mixed Traffic. B—Branch. *See last column.*

Date	CLASS. Name	CLASS. No.	Type	CYLINDERS. No.	CYLINDERS. Diam. and Stroke	Boiler Pres. lbs. per sq. in.	Diam. of Coupled Wheels	
					ins.		ft.ins.	
1923		5205	2-8T-0	2 outs.	19 ×30	200	4 7½	G
1923	Caerphilly Castle	4073	4-6-0	4	16 ×26	225	6 8½	P
1924		5600	0-6-2T	2 ins.	18 ×26	200	4 7½	M
1925	Saint Martin reb'lt	2925	4-6-0	2 outs.	18½×30	225	6 0	P
1927	King	6000	4-6-0	4	16p×28	250	6 6	P
1928	Hall	4901	4-6-0	2 outs.	18½×30	225	6 0	P
1929		5700	0-6-0T	2 ins.	17½×24	200	4 7½	G
1929		5101	2-6-2T	2 outs.	18 ×30	200	5 8	M
1930		2251	0-6-0	2 ins.	17½×24	200	5 2	M
1931		6100	2-6-2T	2 outs.	18 ×30	225	5 8	M
1932		5400	0-6-0T	2 ins.	16½×24	165	5 2	B
1932		6400	0-6-0T	2 ins.	16½×24	165	4 7½	B
1932		4800	0-4-2T	2 ins.	16 ×24	165	5 2	B
1933		9700	0-6-0T	2 ins.	17½×24	200	4 7½	G
1934		1366	0-6-0T	2 outs.	16 ×20	165	3 8	G
1934		7200	2-8-2T	2 outs.	19 ×30	200	4 7½	G
1936	Grange ..	6800	4-6-0	2 outs.	18½×30	225	5 8	M
1936	Earl	3200	4-4-0	2 ins.	18 ×26	180	5 8	P

We ought specially to notice the "5100" and "6100" classes of 2–6–2T locomotives introduced in 1929 and 1931 for suburban passenger services. These engines have cylinders 18 ins. by 30 ins., coupled wheels of 5 ft. 8 ins. diameter, and while the earlier engines had a boiler pressure of 200 lbs., this has been increased in the "6100" class to 225 lbs.

The "7200" class of 2–8–2T engines is also of special interest. These were built as 2–8–0T's ("5200" class), being specially designed for dealing with South Wales coal traffic from pit to port, but with the falling off in the coal export trade some of these engines have been converted to

"7200" Class (2–8–2T)

2–8–2T type with large coal and water capacity, making them suitable for main line freight train services. They are the largest tank engines on the Great Western Railway being 44 ft. 10 ins. over the buffers.

The year 1936 has witnessed the introduction of the "Earl" class (4–4–0 type) engines which are being put into service over routes of the late Cambrian Railway, where the nature of the track imposes a limit on maximum axle loads.

They have driving wheels of 5 ft. 8 ins. diameter, and cylinders of 18 ins. diameter by 26 ins. stroke ; the boiler supplying superheated steam at a pressure of 180 lbs. per square inch. These engines, which have a tractive effort of 18,955 lbs., are somewhat similar to the well known " Duke " class which they will replace.

What's that ? Yes, I knew what you were going to say, that in the story of locomotive progress from 1922 to date I have omitted the most important happening of all, and said nothing about the famous " King " class engines. You have been very patient, I know, but the coming of the *Kings* was such an important event in loco- motive history that I have reserved a separate talk for those mighty engines—which shall be our very next.

"King George V" (No. 6000)—The prototype of the "King" Class of four-cylinder (4–6–0) Express Passenger Locomotives

TALK NUMBER ELEVEN

THE MIGHTY "KINGS"

FOUR years after the first of the "Castle" class engines made its appearance, Mr. Collett produced *King George V* (No. 6000), the first of the four-cylinder 4–6–0 type locomotives of the "King" class. The outstanding feature of this now famous engine was its great hauling power, the tractive effort (at 85 per cent. of the boiler pressure) being no less than 40,300 lbs., which was considerably higher than that of any other passenger locomotive in Great Britain and equivalent to a draw-bar pull of about eighteen tons. Incidentally, the tractive effort of the "King" class engines was 27 per cent. higher than that of the "Castle" class, which had so recently ranked as the most powerful passenger train engines in the country.

You may quite reasonably ask why, with locomotives as fast and powerful as the *Castles* available, the Great Western Railway wanted engines of even greater power. Well, the answer is to be found in the following little table, which gives the maximum loads laid down for passenger trains between Paddington and Plymouth for each of the G.W.R. four-cylinder 4–6–0 types of engine.

Class of Engine.	Paddington to Taunton and back.	Taunton to Plymouth and back.
	tons.	tons.
" King " ..	500	360
" Castle " ..	455	315
" Star " ..	420	288

As you see, between Paddington and Taunton, the *Kings* can take loads 45 tons greater than the *Castles* and 80 tons greater than the *Stars*, while on that section of line between Taunton and Plymouth, which, as you know contains some of the steepest gradients in the country, the power of the *Kings* enables train loads to be increased by 45 tons and 72 tons over the *Castles* and *Stars* respectively.

On its very first run to the West of England, *King George V* climbed the Dainton and Rattery Banks (whose acquaintance you have already made*) unassisted with a train of 338 tons, excluding passengers and luggage, which was at that time the heaviest passenger train load ever worked over the Dainton and Rattery Banks by a single engine.

While still on this point of the high power of the *Kings* you may like to see how they compare with the " Star and " Castle " class engines in respect of weight and tractive effort. Here is a table giving the information, showing that whilst the weight of the engine and tender has increased from the " Star " class of 115 tons 12 cwts.

---

*See " Track Topics."

DIAGRAM OF G.W.R. FOUR-CYLINDER (4-6-0) "KING" CLASS LOCOMOTIVE

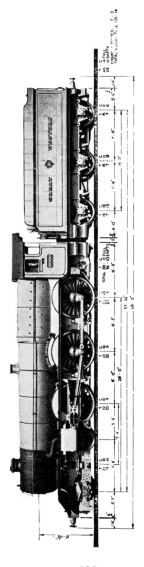

DESCRIPTION

CYLINDERS (FOUR)—Dia. 16¼", Stroke 28".

BOILER—Barrel, length, 16', 0"; Dia. Outs., 6' 0" and 5' 6¼".

Firebox—Length outs, 11' 6".

HEATING SURFACE—2,514 sq. ft. total.

AREA OF FIREGRATE—34.3 sq. ft.

WHEELS—Bogie, 3' 0" ;Coupled, 6' 6".

WATER CAPACITY (TENDER)—4,000 gallons.

WORKING PRESSURE—250 lbs. sq. in.

TRACTIVE EFFORT—40,300 lbs.

to the " King " class of 135 tons 14 cwts., i.e. about $17\frac{1}{2}$ per cent., the tractive effort has increased from 25,085 lbs. to 40,300 lbs. which is 60 per cent.

Date.	Class.	Tractive effort.	Weight of engine and tender.	
		lbs.	tons.	cwts.
1907	" Dog Star "	25,085	115	12
1913	" Prince of Wales " ..	27,800	115	12
1923	" Caerphilly Castle " ..	31,625	119	17
1927	" King George V " ..	40,300	135	14

The weight of a " King " class engine in working order is 89 tons of which 67 tons 10 cwts. is carried on the coupled wheels and the remaining 21 tons 10 cwts. on the bogie. The weight available for adhesion on each of the three driving axles is therefore 22 tons 10 cwts., a figure which exceeds that previously permitted. I may add that some years prior to the coming of the *Kings* a programme of strengthening permanent-way structures had been going on.

The tender used with the " King " class locomotives is of a standard type fitted with water pick-up apparatus. It has a water capacity of 4,000 gallons, carries six tons of coal, weighs 46 tons 14 cwts. when full and 22 tons 10 cwts. when empty. This standard type tender, by the way, is also now used with " Castle " and " Hall " class engines and is described as " self-trimming," that is, the coal automatically feeds to the front of the tender. This is attained by correctly sloping the coal plates.

As compared with *Castles* the cylinder dimensions were increased in the *Kings* from 16 ins. to $16\frac{1}{4}$ ins. diameter, and the piston stroke from 26 ins. to 28 ins. As in the case of other four-cylinder engines, the four cylinders are not set in line across the engine, and are so arranged as to divide the drive between the first and second coupled axles, the inside pair of cylinders driving the leading coupled wheels and the outside pair, the second or middle coupled wheels.

To provide for the increased steam consumption of these larger cylinders a new high-pressure superheater boiler (Standard No. 12) with greater heating surface and firegrate area was designed. The overall length of the firebox was increased to 11 ft. 6 ins. thus making it possible to obtain a firegrate area of 34.3 sq. ft. The total heating surface of the " King " class boiler is 2,514 sq. ft. compared with 2,312 sq. ft. of the " Castle " class.

In the " King " class engines the boiler pressure has been raised to the exceptional figure of 250 lbs. per square inch, the highest working pressure of any railway locomotive boiler of orthodox design, and this has enabled further economies in the use of steam to be effected. The overall length of the boiler is 27 ft. 6 ins., being 2 ft. 8 ins. more than that of the " Castle " class, and this has necessitated an increase in the length of the coupled wheel base from 14 ft. 9 ins. in the " Castle " class engines to 16 ft. 3 ins. in the " King " class.

The diameter of the driving wheels has been reduced to 6 ft. 6 ins. (as compared with the 6 ft. $8\frac{1}{2}$ ins. driving wheels of the *Castles*) resulting in a slight gain in tractive effort, and enabling the engine to maintain a high average speed up steep inclines without seriously affecting the maximum speeds on level stretches or on falling gradients.

The bogie of the " King " class engines, which is spring-controlled, is of new and unique design, having outside bearings on the leading axle and inside bearings on the trailing axle. This feature is necessitated by the desire to have independent springing for each of the bogie wheels, and for this reason the springs on the leading wheels are placed outside the bogie frame, so as to clear the inside cylinders which are placed well forward. The springs on the trailing wheels are placed on the inside of the bogie frame to clear the outside cylinders. The length of the bogie wheel-base is 7 ft. 8 ins.

You are already familiar with the smart appearance of the " King " class of locomotives, and I need not do more, perhaps, than mention the polished brass beadings on cab and splashers, copper-topped chimney, and the artistically lined-out panels and boiler bands. As the tenders pass through the shops the old and familiar lettering " Great Western " with the Company's coat of arms in between the words, hitherto carried on the sides, is being replaced by the newer standard monogram. This applies to all locomotive tenders.

" King " class engines are now employed on many of the principal main line services between London and the West of England via either Westbury or Bristol, as far as Plymouth (including the famous *Cornish Riviera Limited*), and on the direct route between London and the Midlands, as far as Wolverhampton.

"King" class locomotives also haul the *Bristolian*, the new express train London to Bristol and back, which was introduced on September 9th, 1935 to commemorate the centenary of the Great Western Railway and Bristol's association with the Railway. The *Bristolian* makes the double journey of 236 miles on week-days (Saturdays excepted) travelling outwards from London at 10.0 a.m. via Bath, and returning from Bristol at 4.30 p.m. via Badminton. The journey in each direction is made in 105 minutes, which gives average speeds of 67.6 and 67.4 miles an hour for the outward and homeward trips respectively.

Some really fine running has been made with this train, and wonderful stories have been going round as to its speed achievements on certain occasions, but here is an extract from the *Railway Gazette*, which says something interesting on the subject :—

"A correspondent who has made ten journeys on the down train records that with one exception the arrival time has never been more than 42 sec. late nor more than 76 sec. early ; the exception in question was on a morning when signal alterations were in progress at Bristol, and although the *Bristolian* came to a stand just outside Temple Meads in 104 min. from Paddington, it was $4\frac{1}{2}$ min. later that it reached the platform. One run included a dead stand for adverse signals at Westbourne Park, but notwithstanding this and other delays, Bristol was reached a minute early, and the net time on this run, allowing for these checks, was 100 min. for the 118.2 miles start to stop. In the ordinary course of the down run, speed remains consistently above the

Interested schoolboys at Swindon Locomotive Works

70 m.p.h. level for 90 miles on end, and the " King " class 4–6–0's are proving themselves just as capable of evenly sustained high speed as the *Castles* have so long displayed on the *Cheltenham Flyer*. On one journey, a remarkable example of acceleration—particularly as the engine was starting " cold "—was given out of Paddington by *King James I* with the customary load of 218 tons, Langley, only 16.2 miles away being passed at 85 m.p.h., and Slough, 18.5 miles, in 17 min. 17 sec. from the start. On another occasion a maximum of 95 m.p.h. was reached in the descent of Dauntsey bank; but on an unchecked run it is easily possible to maintain the 105 min. schedule without even touching 80 m.p.h."

Preparing a " King " for the run

" King George V." in U.S.A.

Soon after *King George V* appeared it was sent to America, in company with the rebuilt *North Star*, as exhibits at the centenary celebrations of the Baltimore and Ohio Railroad. This exhibition was open to the public from September 24th to October 15th, 1927 and was visited by over a million and a quarter people. *King George V* led the procession of big engines, and was accorded a great reception on every occasion.

After the close of the exhibition and before returning to England, arrangements were made to run the engine on the B. & O. Railroad track and a trip was arranged between Washington and Philadelphia with a train weighing 543.6 tons. Although the fuel supplied was not suitable for the type of grate fitted on the " King " class engines, *King George V* put up a good performance and easily attained over seventy miles an hour, before speed was checked.

Might and majesty—a " King " Class Locomotive

King George V was awarded the medals struck in commemoration of the Baltimore and Ohio Railroad centenary and was also presented with a large brass bell similar to those carried on American locomotives. The engine now carries the medals on the side of the cab and the bell on the buffer plate.

As was fitting, the first " King " class locomotive was named after the then reigning monarch, *King George V* (No. 6000). The other engines in the class have been named after kings of England, working backwards and, as the number is now thirty, the names of all our kings back to King Henry II are represented.

You can, of course, recite their names (and dates) from memory, but here is a list of the names of the engines of the " King " class with their numbers :—

No.	Name.	No.	Name.
6000	King George V	6015	King Richard III
6001	King Edward VII	6016	King Edward V
6002	King William IV	6017	King Edward IV
6003	King George IV	6018	King Henry VI
6004	King George III	6019	King Henry V
6005	King George II	6020	King Henry IV
6006	King George I	6021	King Richard II
6007	King William III	6022	King Edward III
6008	King James II	6023	King Edward II
6009	King Charles II	6024	King Edward I
6010	King Charles I	6025	King Henry III
6011	King James I	6026	King John
6012	King Edward VI	6027	King Richard I
6013	King Henry VIII	6028	King Henry II
6014	King Henry VII	6029	King Edward VIII

Quite recently His Majesty the King graciously consented to the latest of the " King " class engines being named after him, and No. 6029 now proudly carries the name-plate of our Sovereign, *King Edward VIII*.

When commencing these talks, I intimated that I intended to show that the *Castles* and *Kings* are the lineal descendants of old *North Star*, and I trust I have succeeded. Anyway, if you will compare, stage by stage, the photographs of locomotives we have been discussing, you will, I think, be able to trace the development.

On this point, however, you may like to know that Mr. Collett, the designer of both the " Castle " and " King " classes of locomotives has said :—

" My ambition was to follow, even if a very long way off, very humbly in the footsteps of the great George Stephenson. . . . at a meeting of the Institution of Mechanical Engineers in London a little while ago the Chairman remarked that the *Castle* engines in use on the Great Western Railway were just like George Stephenson's. I do not think he meant that for praise, but to my mind he could not have paid us a greater compliment, and I hope and trust that the engines of the new ' King ' class will prove to be also just as if George Stephenson had built them."

And to *that* I can usefully add—nothing at all.

Ever since the introduction of the " King " class of locomotives the keenest interest has been displayed all over the world in the performance of these engines. Reproductions in miniature have been in constant demand, and no model railway system has been considered really complete, or up-to-date, unless equipped with its G.W.R. " King " class engine.

"King Richard III" (No. 6015).

Excursion trains to Swindon Works—"the birth-place of the *Kings*"—have been organised on numerous occasions, particularly during school holiday periods, from London and many provincial centres. These trips have been arranged at an inclusive fare covering the return railway journey and a conducted tour of the locomotive workshops at Swindon, where many thousands of "boys of all ages" have been entranced and intrigued by demonstrations of the modern mechanical processes which go to the making of *Kings*, *Castles*, and other G.W.R. locomotives.

"King" class engines have, quite appropriately, been employed in hauling these excursion trains, and this feature has added considerably to the interest and enjoyment of many young railway speed enthusiasts, for the *Kings* have been out to show their paces, and remarkably good running has been accomplished on some of these trips.

" 5700 " Class (0–6–0T)

TALK NUMBER TWELVE

TRACTIVE EFFORT AND CLASSIFICATION

SEVERAL times we have used the term " tractive effort," particularly in regard to the " King " class of locomotives, and I think it is high time that I redeemed my promise to explain more particularly what this term means.

The force which a locomotive exerts in hauling a load is referred to as its " tractive effort " and the maximum force thus exerted—that required at the moment of starting—is generally accepted as the basis for comparing the capacity of different locomotives for their respective duties.

Five factors have to be considered in determining this maximum. They are :—

(a) the number of cylinders,

(b) the diameter of the cylinders,

(c) the length of the piston stroke,

(d) the diameter of the driving wheels, and

(e) the pressure of steam acting on the pistons.

It is fairly obvious that the larger the number of cylinders and the greater their diameter and length of piston stroke, the greater must be the tractive effort, but perhaps the effect of the diameter of the driving wheels is not so apparent.

You will be aware that when a motor car has to ascend a hill, or is called on for other hard work, it is put into low

gear in order to get a greater turning effort or " pull."
The effect of this is similar to reducing the diameter of the
wheels, as for the same number of revolutions of the engine,
the car covers a smaller distance. Although there are no
intermediate gears in a railway locomotive, the same
principle applies. Consequently if two engines are iden-
tical in all other respects, but have driving wheels of
different diameters, the engine with the smaller wheels will
have the greater tractive effort, although, of course, with
each revolution it will cover less ground.

This difference in the diameter of the driving wheels
constitutes the essential difference between passenger and
freight locomotives. The former haul comparatively
light loads, but are required to travel at high speeds, and
so are equipped with wheels of large diameter ; the latter,
however, are required to haul heavier loads at comparatively low speeds, and are thus provided with small
diameter wheels.

That is fairly clear, I hope, but you will probably say
" What about the effect of steam pressure ? "

Well, the higher the steam pressure, of course, the
greater the tractive effort. I should, however, point out
that for two reasons only a certain percentage of the full
boiler pressure is taken into account. Firstly, when
the engine is in full gear, giving maximum opening
to the valves, steam is cut off at about 75 per cent.
of the piston stroke, after which point it expands and
fills the cylinder behind the moving piston, but its
pressure drops. Secondly, there is necessarily a fall in
pressure between boiler steam and valve chest steam.
The result of these two facts is that at starting the

" 4300 " Class (2–6–0)

" 4700 " Class (2–8–0)

" 5200 " Class (2–8–0T)

average pressure on the piston head is about 85 per cent. of the boiler pressure.

The combined effect of these various factors is expressed in a formula which gives the tractive effort of any locomotive in pounds (lbs.).

Here is the formula :—

$$\text{tractive effort} = \frac{n}{2} \times \frac{0.85p \times d^2 \times l}{D} \text{ lb.}$$

where
- n = number of cylinders.
- p = boiler pressure in lb. per sq. in.
- d = diameter of cylinders in inches.
- l = length of stroke in inches.
- D = diameter of driving wheels in inches.

As a railway locomotive enthusiast, I think you might like to keep that formula by you, but if you care to insert the appropriate figures in respect of the " King " class of locomotives, you will find that the tractive effort works out at 40,300 lbs., which is more than four times that of *Lord of the Isles*. We have said before that the tractive effort of the *Kings* is about 27 per cent. more than that of the *Castles* and this, of course, is due to the fact that whilst boiler pressure, cylinder diameter and stroke are all higher, the diameter of the driving wheels (the divisor) is slightly lower.

On Great Western Railway locomotives, a letter is painted on the side of the cab which denotes to the initiated within what limits the tractive effort of a locomotive falls, and tractive effort is, of course, one means of classifying locomotives for various duties.

TRACTIVE EFFORT AND CLASSIFICATION

You asked " What is the horse-power of a railway loco-motive ? " Well, that all depends on what you mean by " horse-power."

The horse-power of motor cars is generally quoted in terms of their maximum continuous out-put, and where the range of power is given as, say, 60–90 h.p., it means that the engine is capable of exerting 60 h.p. continuously and 90 h.p. for short periods under specified conditions only.

Whilst it is not possible to apply a fixed " horse-power " rating to locomotives as is usual with motor-cars, it may be said that a " King " class engine would exert about 2,000 h.p. under maximum conditions and about 1,200 h.p. continuously.

Horse-powers as high, and higher, than that are of course developed by internal combustion engines, par-ticularly in aircraft, but these are engines revolving at extremely high speeds and, therefore, the tractive force is correspondingly low. Such engines, despite their high horse-power, would not be much use for starting a train like *Cornish Riviera Limited* from rest with its load of about 500 tons behind the tender ; the job which a " King " class engine tackles with ease as part of its daily routine.

ა   ა   ა   ა

Now we are on this question of classification, we might consider it a little more fully. There are, as you know, three main classes of locomotives which may be divided as follows :—

PASSENGER : express, semi-express, stopping, suburban or branch trains.

GOODS : fast vacuum fitted, ordinary goods and mineral trains.

SHUNTING : for work in goods yards and docks.

Classification does not impose any hard and fast rule on the class of work of locomotives. There are occasions when passenger engines are used to work goods trains or when shunting engines are employed on local passenger trains and so on. From what has been said, however, I think it will be clear that classification assists in selecting an engine for a particular job, bearing in mind such factors as the nature of traffic, the load to be hauled, the speed at which the train must be run, ruling gradients, etc.

You have already made the acquaintance of the numeral system of classifying engines by their wheel arrangement. This system, which hails from America, is now almost universal. You will recall that the three numerals in their order, beginning with the front of the engines, signify, first, the leading or carrying wheels, a pair (pony truck) or four (bogie) ; the second numeral indicates the number of driving or coupled wheels ; and the last numeral represents the number of carrying wheels or trailers behind the drivers.

Thus, 4–6–0 represents a ten-wheeled engine with a leading bogie (4 wheels), six coupled driving wheels and no trailing wheels—4+6+0=10.

Because this system of classification takes no account of the tender, the letter T is added to distinguish tank engines —thus 2–8–0T.

TRACTIVE EFFORT AND CLASSIFICATION

Locomotives may be classified, according to their wheel arrangements, into the following four main groups.

1. All wheels coupled.
2. Carrying wheels in front of coupled wheels.
3. Carrying wheels behind coupled wheels.
4. Carrying wheels in front of and behind coupled wheels.

Let me give you a brief description of some of the G.W.R. engines in each of these classes, and here are photographs of various types which you can look at meanwhile.

ALL WHEELS COUPLED TOGETHER.

The types of engine in this group consist mainly of 0–6–0T (six wheels coupled tank engines) used for shunting, etc. This wheel arrangement is particularly suitable for moving heavy loads, as the whole of the weight of the engine is available for adhesion. Engines of this type are designed with smaller diameter wheels to give the necessary tractive force, and this makes them unsuitable for fast running. These engines are the " handy-men " of the fleet, and can take on almost any job within their power, at short notice. But in saying this I do not, of course, mean that they could haul the *Cornish Riviera Limited*, or a thousand-tons mineral train.

CARRYING WHEELS IN FRONT OF COUPLED WHEELS

2–6–0.—These six wheels coupled engines with a leading pony truck are provided with 4 ft. $7\frac{1}{2}$ ins. diameter wheels for freight work. They superseded the six-wheels coupled (0–6–0) engines for this work, and supplied the increased power required for present-day heavy loads.

" 5400 " Class (0–6–0T)

" 4500 " Class (2-6-2T)

"3150" Class (2–6–2T)

"4800" Class (0–4–2T)

"5600" Class (0–6–2T

2–8–0 or " Consolidation " type.—These tender engines (eight wheels coupled with a leading pony truck) are provided with 4 ft. 7½ ins. diameter wheels, and are designed for heavy mineral traffic. The extra pair of coupled wheels enables a larger boiler to be carried. An example of this type of engine is the " 2800 " class.

2–8–0T.—The " 4200 " class of Great Western engine represents the " Consolidation " tank engine, and is built on the lines of the " 2800 " class. It has, however, a smaller boiler and side tanks and bunker instead of a tender. These are extremely useful engines for " banking " purposes, and for moving heavy mineral trains in congested districts.

2–6–0 " Mixed traffic " engine.—This engine is not required to run as fast as the express passenger engine with 6 ft. 8½ ins. wheels, and its wheels are, therefore, of medium size (5 ft. 8 ins.), which enables a fairly fast speed to be attained on passenger trains and sufficient power to be developed to work fairly heavy freight trains. These engines are particularly useful when required to work over a route with severe gradients. They are represented by the " 4300 " class.

2–8–0 " Mixed traffic " engine.—These engines ("4700 " class) are exceptional, as they are the only representatives of their class in this country with 5 ft. 8 in. coupled wheels. The larger boiler carried by these engines necessitated the use of an extra pair of coupled wheels, thereby increasing the adhesive power and enabling them to haul heavier loads.

4–4–0 type.—These engines (four wheels coupled with a leading bogie) were for a long time the standard for express passenger work, and are still used for this purpose on lines where heavier engines cannot be utilised. They have done splendid work, and with medium loads can still put up some fine performances. Typical 4–4–0 engines are those of the old " Duke " and " Bulldog " classes, both of which have 5 ft. 8 in. driving wheels.

4–6–0 type.—This important type of engine (six wheels coupled with leading bogie) has now largely taken the place of the 4–4–0 type for express passenger trains, on account of the adhesion obtained with the additional pair of coupled wheels and the larger boiler which can be carried. The four-cylinder " 4000 " class and the two-cylinder " 2900 " class on the Great Western are typical examples of this type of engine. As you already know the four-cylinder 4–6–0 type includes the " Star," " Castle," and " King " classes of engines, and the two-cylinder 4–6–0 type the " Saint " and " Hall " classes.

CARRYING WHEELS BEHIND THE COUPLED WHEELS

Included in this group are the 0–4–2T and 0–6–2T types of engines. The former was designed for passenger traffic and is still used for this purpose, but increasing loads make these engines unsuitable for main line traffic. Nowadays they are usually employed on branch lines and similar light work.

The 0–6–2T is a development of the 0–6–0T and performs the same duties, the additional pair of trailing carrying wheels having been provided to accommodate a larger bunker and tanks. Engines of these groups include the " 5600 " class and are extensively used in South Wales.

CARRYING WHEELS IN FRONT OF AND BEHIND COUPLED WHEELS

2–6–2T.—These are powerful six-wheels coupled tank engines represented by the " 3150 " and the " 5100 " classes, which have 5 ft. 8 in. diameter coupled wheels, and can, therefore, be employed on freight and passenger work. They may be classified as a " mixed traffic " tank engines.

These tank engines are usually termed " double enders " as they are designed to run in either direction. By carrying coal and water on the same frame as the engine, the cost of a separate tender is avoided, and as it is not necessary to turn the engine at the end of each journey, much trouble is avoided.

2–8–2T.—You have already been told something of these locomotives (" 7200 " class) which were conversions of the 2–8–0T type. These may be regarded as more powerful versions of the 2–6–2T locomotives. They have driving wheels of 4 ft. 7½ ins. diameter, and are employed on heavy main line freight services.

၄ ၄ ၄ ၄

I do not propose to say much about the question of engine names and numbers beyond the fact that as the Great Western Railway publishes a useful little book on this subject,* but you will already have observed that the names of passenger locomotives are in classes and are selected on a

---

*" Great Western Railway Engines : Names, Numbers, Types, and Classes " (1s.). Published by The Great Western Railway, Paddington Station, London, W 2

systematic basis, having a parent name common to the class, and an individual name; e.g. engines of the "Castle" class are named *Windsor Castle, Caerphilly Castle, Manorbier Castle* and so on. Perhaps, however, I ought to add that whilst passenger engines bear names and numbers, goods engines are nowadays only numbered.

And now, if there are no questions you wish to ask about tractive force or the classification of locomotives, we will proceed to consider, in turn, the various components of the engine and boiler.

In these talks I try to keep in mind the fact that, being something of a railway enthusiast, you already know a good deal about some of the matters discussed. I should not like you to think that I was " talking-down " to you in any way, nor that you were possibly saying to yourself :—

> " Teach not a parent's mother to extract
> The embryo juices of an egg by suction,
> The good old lady can this feat enact
> Quite irrespective of your kind instruction ! "

—or more familiar words to that effect.

Main frames in Slotting Machine

TALK NUMBER THIRTEEN

THE ENGINE COMPONENTS

WE have now traced the locomotive history of the Great Western Railway over a period of a hundred years and discussed the principal types of engines, their essential features and functions, and I think we might profitably consider the components of the locomotive.

We may as well select the most powerful while we are about it, so I suggest we turn our attention to the principal parts of the " King " class of locomotives. We will begin with the engine proper, and in this connection a few photographs and drawings will assist us and save a good many words. Here we go then.

THE MAIN FRAMES

We will make a start with the main frames of the locomotives. They come from the maker in the form of long rectangular slabs of steel 41 ft. 4 in. in length, by 3 ft. 6 ins. in width, and 1¼ ins. thick. These are first of all roughly punched to shape and, after annealing and levelling, are assembled in lots of eight or ten and machined to the finished dimensions in a slotting machine.

The next process is the " dishing " of the frames at the leading end in order to provide clearance for the movement of the bogie wheels. This is done in powerful hydraulic presses and the frames are afterwards drilled as required in pairs.

Main frames—cutting by Oxygen-Coal Gas Jet Frame Cutting Machine

THE CYLINDERS

As you already know, the " King " class of engine has four cylinders (two outside and two inside), and these comprise three separate castings ; the two inside cylinders form one casting carrying a portion of the saddle for supporting the smoke-box, and each of the two outside cylinders is cast separately.   The steam chest in each case (which are in effect smaller cylinders in which two piston valves mounted on a spindle control the entry of steam to alternate ends of the cylinders) are embodied in the respective cylinder castings.   Passages are provided in all the cylinders for tapping off a certain proportion of the exhaust steam for use in working the exhaust steam injector (to which we shall refer presently).

When we visited Swindon Works on the occasion of our *Cheltenham Flyer* trip, we spent some time in the Iron Foundry and saw the molten metal used for cylinder castings, in the cupolas and being conveyed by overhead

cranes in huge ladles to the moulds, waiting to receive it.*
As then explained to you, when pouring the metal, the
bores of the cylinder, steam chest, etc., are taken up
by "cores" which have to be broken up and removed
from the casting when completed. For such a casting as

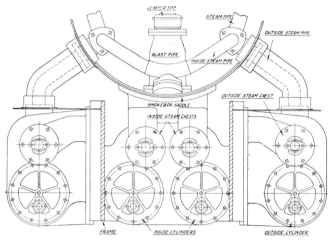

Diagram of Cylinders

the combined inside cylinders and saddle no less than
twenty cores are required, and the moulding box has to be
built in four separate portions.

After the castings have been removed from the moulds,
they go to the Cylinder Machine Shop, where the sides
of the cylinders and the radius face of the smoke-box
saddle are carefully machined, and the steam chests bored

---

*See "Cheltenham Flyer."

to receive the piston valve bushes. This latter operation is carried out in a special machine which deals with all four of the inside cylinder bushes at one time.

A battery of machines for drilling and tapping the various bolt and stud holes is included in the equipment of the cylinder-machining shop and you may be surprised to learn that the capacity of the shop is 262 pairs of cylinders per annum.

THE PISTONS

The piston head, a hollow iron casting of the " box " type, is secured to the piston rod (turned from the best rolled steel bar) by means of a tapered screw thread and dowel, thereby preserving a flat face to the front of the piston head and enabling the cylinder cover to be of strong and simple design.

The piston head contains two grooves in which are fitted the piston rings, which expand evenly against the cylinder walls, as in a motor cycle engine, thus ensuring steam

Cylinder Castings—pair of inside cylinders on right, outside cylinder on le

Planing two inside cylinders

tightness. The piston rod is kept steam-tight in passing through the back cylinder cover by means of a stuffing box and gland. Flexible metallic packing covered with

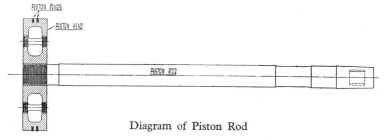

Diagram of Piston Rod

graphite paste is pressed into the stuffing box tightly enough to prevent leakage of steam without scoring the rod.

THE CROSSHEADS

The crossheads are steel castings in which the slippers are incorporated. The faces of the slippers are lined with anti-friction metal held in position by means of corrugations in the face of the slipper. Bronze safety strips are let in so that should the white metal get hot and run out no damage will be done. A 50-ton press is employed to force the crosshead on to the piston rod and a special broaching machine cuts out the hole for the cotter with the two units so assembled, thus securing perfect alignment.

The Connecting and Coupling Rods

The connecting rods, which transmit the motion of the crossheads to the crank pins, and the coupling rods, which

are the means of harnessing the adhesive weight of the engine, are both machined from forgings of the highest quality carbon steel to an ⊥ section giving maximum strength with a minimum weight of material. The holes for the bushes at the ends of the rods are ground out to the finished dimensions.

Cranked Axle

THE AXLE BOXES

The driving axle boxes are steel castings into which are pressed gun-metal liners with white metal cast on the bearing surfaces. Oil is supplied to the horn cheeks and to the top of the journal by means of pipes leading from oil boxes carried on the frames, and fed to the bottom of the journal by pads saturated with oil and pressed against the journal by springs. This diagram, I think, makes it clear.

THE AXLES

The cranked axle, on to which the inside cylinders drive, is built up from steel slabs and forged steel bars. The slabs are planed and bored to form the webs and are shrunk on to the bars, which are turned to form the crank pins and shaft. The other axles are straight, the crank

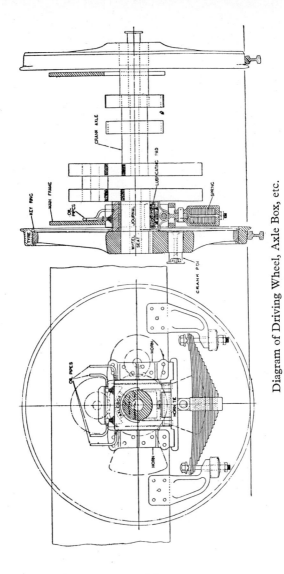

Diagram of Driving Wheel, Axle Box, etc.

166

pins and coupling rods being forced into the bosses of the wheel centres by hydraulic pressure.

THE WHEELS

You had a complete demonstration at the Swindon Works on our *Cheltenham Flyer* trip of the various operations involved in the preparation of a pair of locomotive wheels.* You will remember that the wheel centres are of cast steel and are bored to receive the ends of the axles on to which they are forced by hydraulic pressure—about 130 tons. A tyre is bored somewhat smaller than the diameter of its wheel centre and is heated in a gas furnace by a series of gas jets until the diameter has increased to something greater than that of the centre. The tyre is then placed over the centre and allowed to shrink so that it grips tightly. A retaining ring is then hammered down between a lip on the tyre and the rim of the wheel centre, in order to hold the tyre in the remote possibility of it ever becoming loose.

The wheels and axle are then taken to a wheel lathe and after the tyre has been turned to the correct profile, the holes which receive the crank pins or coupling-rod pins are bored out in a quartering machine. This machine has two heads arranged at right angles so that both wheels can be bored simultaneously and at the correct angle. The wheels and axle finally go to a specially designed machine in which they are correctly balanced at speeds representing 60 miles per hour on the rail.

---

*See " Cheltenham Flyer.

THE VALVE GEAR

You already know something about valve gears although admittedly the subject is a rather intricate one to explain briefly. In the " King " class engines the piston valves of the inside cylinders are driven directly by Walschaërts' gear, with which you are already familiar. The gear gives a motion compounded of two distinct movements. The principal movement is derived from an eccentric keyed to

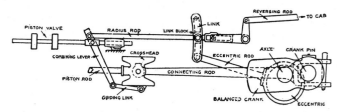

Diagram of Walschaërt valve gear

the axle and the other movement from a connection taken from the crosshead. These two movements are conveyed one to each end of a combining lever on which is a third point driving the valve spindle. This gear is adopted because of the relative lightness of its moving parts and its special suitability for high speeds.

The motion for the valves of the outside cylinders is derived from that of the inside by means of horizontal rocking levers carried on pivots fitted to the engine frames.

I am afraid that is brief indeed, but the subject is one rather difficult to describe simply in few words. Here is a diagram (which you have seen before) of Walschaërts' gear and this will help to illustrate my points.

THE ENGINE COMPONENTS

THE INJECTORS

The injector is a means of feeding hot water into the boiler against the steam pressure therein. Two injectors are always carried below the footplate, one on either side of the engine, and are operated from the cab.

A locomotive boiler will evaporate from three to seven tons of water per hour according to its size, and this quantity must be forced into the boiler with certainty and regularity as required.

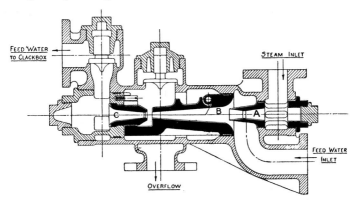

Arrangement of cones in live steam injector

For locomotive purposes there are two types : live steam restarting injectors, and exhaust restarting injectors. The former is worked entirely by live steam from the boiler and is fitted on the right-hand side of all G.W.R. engines. The exhaust injector utilises exhaust steam from the cylinders together with a small supply of live steam from the boiler. If desired this injector can also be worked by live steam

alone. It is fitted on the left-hand side of all express passenger engines, and large type goods engines. When no
exhaust injector is fitted, two live steam restarting injectors
are used.

The action of both injectors is the same. Steam is
passed through a small tapering nozzle, so forming a high
velocity steam jet which is led through a conical water space,
where the steam is condensed, thus creating a vacuum
in the body of the injector. The formation of this vacuum
causes the boiler steam to expand with a high velocity
which is imparted to the water column, which then passes
through a delivery cone of increasing diameter. In the
delivery cone the velocity, or rather what our technical
friends more correctly term the " kinetic energy " of the
water, changes to pressure energy, ultimately sufficient
to overcome the boiler pressure and to open what is called
the " clack " valve in the feed pipe to the boiler.

THE LUBRICATORS

You had better look closely at this diagram of the
Swindon triple sight-feed lubricator, if you want to know
how this ingenious apparatus works.

Lubrication is effected by feeding cylinder oil into the
steam in the regulator box (pipe S) and to the cylinders
(pipe F). The oil contained in the lubricator is displaced
through the sight-feed glasses by steam from the boiler
condensing in pipes C. The feed to the cylinders is
taken through D to a combining valve W. (I hope you
can follow this).

Here the oil is mixed with steam from the boiler and is carried along pipe F to the steam pipes in the smokebox

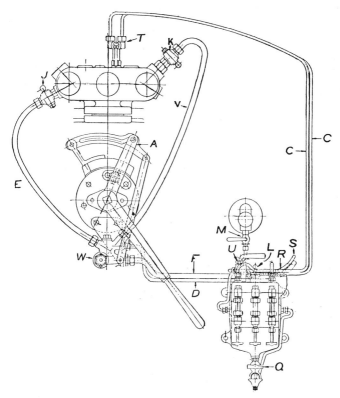

"Swindon" Triple Sight-Feed Lubricator

and thence to the cylinders. Valve W, which is operated by moving the regulator handle, is so arranged that oil is fed to the cylinders when the engine is "drifting" (or "coasting") and the regulator valve is shut.

In cold weather, steam may be passed through the body of the lubricator to warm the oil by opening the valve marked M.

໙ ໙ ໙ ໙

Well, that, I hope, is a helpful, if somewhat abridged, description of some of the principal engine components. The engine may be referred to as the steam user and in our next talk we will discuss the important duties of the steam producer, that is, the boiler.

TALK NUMBER FOURTEEN

THE BOILER COMPONENTS

A T Swindon Works they pride themselves, quite justifiably, on the excellence of their boiler construction. To the lay mind the boiler, on account of its size, is probably the most impressive part of a locomotive; anyway, it is true to say that the efficiency of the locomotive is dependent more upon its boiler than on any other part. When speaking of the boiler, by the way, the fire-box, smoke-box and other adjuncts are generally included.

Now the requirements of a locomotive boiler are many. It must raise quickly and efficiently a sufficient volume of steam to meet the requirements of the engine under all conditions of working. It must be so designed as to withstand safely a pressure considerably in excess of that at which it normally works, and every provision must be made for quick and thorough cleaning at frequent intervals so that the efficiency of the heat transmitting surfaces remains unimpaired throughout their working life.

It must afford every facility for the most economic consumption of the fuel provided, and for transferring the maximum heat generated to the water and steam. With all this, it must conform to the restrictions of space imposed by the various structures met with on the railway and by those of the engine frames upon which it is carried. Further, due regard must also be paid to the manner in which the total weight of the boiler is distributed over the wheels of the engine.

The characteristic feature of the G.W.R. standard boiler is the coning of the barrel. Introduced, as we have seen, in 1903, the coning was first restricted to the back barrel ring, but was later extended to the whole length of the barrel in order still further to improve the circulation of the water in the boiler. We have already seen how the tapering of the barrel enables the fullest use to be made of the intense heat in the neighbourhood of the firebox end, and how it minimises the danger of uncovering the firebox crown plates.

The steam generated in the boiler is collected by an internal pipe with an upturned mouth placed above the top of the front end of the firebox, thus ensuring that dry steam only is taken to the regulator or main steam valve. This arrangement enables the latter to be placed in the smokebox, where it is readily accessible. At the same time the position of the collector pipe obviates the need for a steam dome, which is a familiar, but not very artistic, feature of many locomotives.

The principal parts of the boiler are the firebox, the barrel, and the smoke-box.

THE FIREBOX

The firebox, in which the fuel is burnt, consists of an inner box of copper surrounded by an outer casing or shell of mild steel plate, the two being connected at the bottom by a heavy steel ring, called the " foundation ring." The inner box is built up from three plates riveted together, the front or tube plate, the back plate, and the wrapper

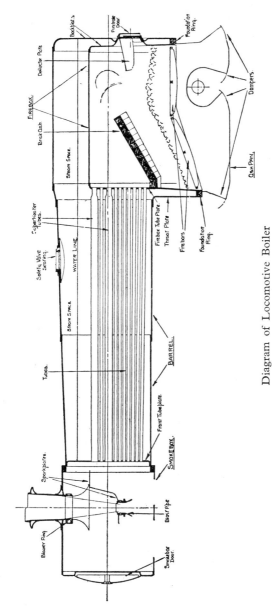

Diagram of Locomotive Boiler

NOTE.—*Superheater, Regulator Box and Gear, Safety Valve, Stays, etc., not shewn.*

plate. In British locomotive practice copper is invariably used for the inner box on account of its greater resistance to the corrosive action of the fire, and its ability to withstand the distortion set up by the high temperatures developed in the firebox.

The outer firebox casing consists of a throat plate, into which one end of the barrel is fitted; a back plate, flanged with the copper back plate to form the firehole and a wrapper plate, which is usually in three portions, one crown sheet and two side sheets, riveted together with butt strips. The throat plate connects the circular barrel to the rectangular-shaped fire-box.

Throat Plate

Among important fittings enclosed in the firebox are the brick arch, the firegrate, and the ashpan.

THE BRICK ARCH

The process of combustion can only proceed satisfactorily providing the surrounding temperature is sufficiently high. It is therefore desirable to maintain a high and consistent furnace temperature in the locomotive firebox. This is aided by the provision of an arch of fire-bricks.

The brick arch extends in an upward direction from just below the bottom row of tubes in the firebox tube plate to about the middle of the firebox. It serves a two-fold purpose, first by delaying the passage of the gases, and second by reflecting them back on to the burning mass in the grate which rapidly approaches incandescence.

Further to assist the combustion of the coal in the firebox some air must be allowed to enter over the top of the fire-bed, and for this reason the firehole doors are cast hollow so that, even when shut, a current of air may be admitted. A deflector plate, fitted inside the firehole, prevents this additional air from impinging directly on the tube plate and thus causing leaky tubes.

The Firegrate

The firegrate is arranged in sections, each consisting of a number of cast-iron firebars carried on transverse supports. Each bar is cast with lugs at the centre and ends which, acting as spacers, ensure that sufficient air space is provided. The front sections slope downwards towards the front of the firebox and, with the vibration of the engine, assist in getting the coal well forward.

The Ashpan

The ashpan, built up from $\frac{3}{16}$ in. steel plate, is secured to the bottom of the foundation ring and is made up in two portions so that, if necessary, it can be readily assembled over the trailing axle, which at this point is shielded from the heat of the fire by an asbestos lagging attached to the ashpan. The four doors provided, called " dampers," can be opened or closed from the footplate, and their adjustment enables the amount of air admitted to the underside of the grate to be controlled.

THE BARREL

The barrel is the large horizontal cylindrical portion of the boiler and is built up from two mild steel plates rolled into butt-jointed circular rings which are riveted together with a circumferential lap joint. The front end is closed by a steel tube plate riveted in position and drilled to receive a large number of steel tubes, $2\frac{1}{4}$ ins. in diameter, through which the hot gases pass on their way to the smokebox. The tubes are expanded into the tube plates at either end of the barrel in order to make them steam-tight, and where there is a risk of corroding deposits accumulating on the projecting ends, the tubes are beaded over to reduce the possibility of subsequent leakage.

The barrel and front tube plate are securely stayed or tied to the firebox and shell by long steel stays, or rods with threaded ends that screw into the plates. The sides and top of the inner and outer firebox are similarly stayed to each other by a number of short steel or copper stays.

You would doubtless like to know something about the effect of steam pressure upon the boiler and why all this " staying " is necessary. Well, the bursting force exerted on the cylindrical " King " class boiler barrel may be as high as 1,500 tons. The flat surfaces of the firebox may be subjected to a pressure load of 1,200 tons, while the crown or roof of the firebox may have to withstand a downward pressure of 820 tons. Hence the need for those numerous steel or copper stays of which there are 2,000 on the firebox alone of a " King " class locomotive.

Equally important to the " staying " of the boiler is the maintenance of correct water level which is indicated by a gauge glass secured in the frame bolted on the back plate of the firebox, and positioned so that at half glass the water level is 5 ins. above the top of the inside firebox.

Although it is a refinement with which we are hardly concerned, I might mention that, as a safety precaution against the very remote possibility of a failure of the feed water supply to the boiler, there is a plug of fusible metal in the top of the firebox which, in the event of the plates not being covered by water when the engine is in steam, would melt and the inrushing steam would put out the fire.

THE SMOKEBOX

The smokebox, cylindrical in shape, is riveted to the front end of the barrel, and with the door, which is of sufficient size to allow the tubes to be withdrawn or cleaned, forms an airtight compartment (with the exception of the chimney opening) through which the products of combustion are drawn on their way to the chimney.

After the steam has performed its useful work in the cylinders, it is exhausted through the blast pipe and chimney to the atmosphere. Some of the air contained in the smokebox is carried out with each jet of steam, and, to take its place, air flows in by way of the firebox and tubes. The blast of the exhaust steam thus produces the intense draught necessary for the combustion of the fuel. When

Starting or when working heavily on an ascending gradient, the volume of steam which is emitted from the blast pipe is so great that it would exert too fierce a pull on the fire, and so an automatic " jumper " top is fitted to the blast pipe. This " jumper " lifts when the exhaust exceeds a

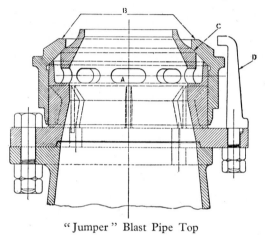

" Jumper " Blast Pipe Top

When working heavily exhaust steam pressure lifts ring B, providing an extra outlet for exhaust through holes A and space between lifted ring B and its seat C. Lift of ring B is limited by stops D.

certain amount and provides an additional exit for the steam, thus softening the effect on the fire.

A spark arrester is fitted in the smokebox to induce an even draught through all the tubes, as, due to the position of the blast pipe top, there is a tendency for an excessive draught to be created through the top tubes. This plate gives the gases a downward trend, with the result that any ash drawn through the tubes is deposited in the bottom of the smokebox, so preventing sparks being thrown from the chimney.

At the base of the chimney is a blower ring. The blower directs live steam from the boiler up the chimney, through a series of inclined holes drilled through the inner wall of the ring. By this means the blower can assist the action of the blast, but is, of course, only used under exceptional running conditions, or when it is necessary to raise steam quickly in the shed.

The regulator box containing the main steam valve and its " jockey " or pilot valve is fixed in the smokebox at the top of the front tube plate and controls the amount of steam admitted to the cylinders. The pilot valve not only permits of a very gradual admission of steam, but also facilitates the opening of the regulators as, with the full steam pressure acting on the valve, it is almost impossible to open the main valve directly.

The remaining important component is the superheater, and in a well-arranged talk, I suppose we should now be considering it, but as its construction and operation have already been explained, we can bring this talk to a close. Having considered the principal parts of the boiler, I want next to have a talk on boiler construction.

Pressing a Throat Plate

Large Bending Rolls

TALK NUMBER FIFTEEN

CONSTRUCTING THE BOILER

AN important feature of Swindon practice has always been the hydraulic flanging of both steel and copper plates. One of the first steps in boiler construction is the preparation of the blocks and dies with which the various shapes are pressed. These blocks are of cast iron and are machined to the finished dimensions so that it is unnecessary to correct the shape of the plates after pressing. A particularly good example of hydraulic flanging is that of the front casing or throat plate which is made from $\frac{3}{4}$ in. mild steel plate and pressed out to its finished form in one heat, and you will readily understand that reduction in the number of heats means both economy in the cost of manufacture and minimum of distortion in the material. Before being used the blocks are warmed up in order to avoid any sudden chilling of the plate as the two come in contact.

If you recall our visit to Swindon Works, you will remember we visited the Boiler Shop—one of the most up-to-date of its kind in existence—and saw the various presses, flame cutting machines, plate rolls, etc., in use.

Two presses are provided in the boiler shop ; the larger of the two (which you see in this photograph) deals with the heaviest classes of flanged plate work, while the smaller is used principally for flanging smokebox tube plates and

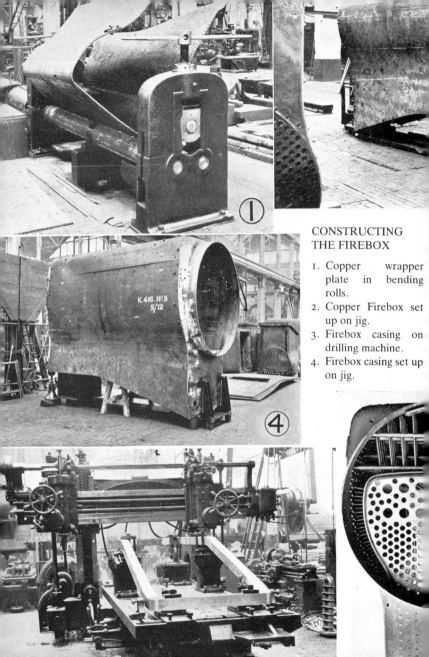

CONSTRUCTING THE FIREBOX

1. Copper wrapper plate in bending rolls.
2. Copper Firebox set up on jig.
3. Firebox casing on drilling machine.
4. Firebox casing set up on jig.

K.416. Nº5
S/12

2. Firebox casing in hydraulic riveting machine.
3. Foundation Ring in drilling machine.
4. Finished Firebox.
5. Foundation Ring being drilled on 8 ft. radial machine.

for levelling smokebox rings. Operating at a pressure of 1,500 lbs. per square inch, the larger press exerts a total pressure of 650 tons, and the other a pressure of about 200 tons.

The heating of the plates preparatory to pressing is carried out in either of two furnaces, the larger of which is coal fired and the other gas fired. The plates are manipulated mechanically when charging and discharging the furnaces with considerable saving in labour and time, besides enabling the work to be carried out with a minimum of physical discomfort to the workmen. The flanging of copper plates " in the cold " by hydraulic pressure, was first carried out successfully at Swindon Works, and, besides being much cheaper than hand flanging results in a big reduction in the number of plates with cracked corners.

After having been in the press, the rough-edged flanges of the steel plates are trimmed to the correct finished dimensions by an oxy-coal gas flame cutter. The copper plates are trimmed in horizontal band-sawing machines, the band-saw being supported in hardened steel guides carried on adjustable sliding brackets which permit of any sized plate being dealt with.

The barrel and wrapper plates are marked out to templates, the outline of the steel plates being cut out by a portable oxy-acetylene flame cutting machine. The stay holes in the crown plates are drilled, together with a few " tacking " holes along the seams, enabling the plates to be bolted together temporarily in assembling. Where one edge of a plate has to butt against another edge, such edges have to be carefully machined, and you will appreciate that very accurate work is required when, for example, the barrel plates are to fit one inside the other.

The copper and steel wrapper plates and the barrel plates are rolled to the correct shape in large bending rolls, three sets of which are used for rolling the plates and one for levelling them. Should the radius which it is desired to roll be smaller than that of the rolls themselves, use is then made of an auxiliary wooden roll placed between the main roll and the plate. The barrel plates are rolled conical throughout their length, but the ends require to be parallel as the rings fit one inside the other. The ends are therefore placed in a press consisting of a central block, the diameter of which is the exact internal diameter of the ring to be pressed, and a series of radial sectors which are pressed inwards with a force of 1,500 lbs. per square inch.

The inner firebox and the outer casing are separately assembled on jigs, the plates being held together temporarily by means of the " tackling bolts " previously mentioned. The jigs can be adjusted to suit the varying heights and lengths of different fireboxes and they have tubular legs which can be let down to support a platform upon which men may carry out work on the top of the box.

The rivet holes along the seams of the copper firebox are drilled while the box is still assembled on its jig, but the outer casing is taken to a special drilling machine. The drilling head of this machine can be raised to any height, and the table, to which the casing is secured, is capable of rotating through any angle and also of traversing in two directions at right angles to one another. With such a machine it is possible to drill the necessary holes however awkward may be their positions.

We are fortunate in having good photographs to illustrate these operations. They almost tell the story themselves.

The various plates are next riveted together, and the outer casing riveted in a powerful hydraulic machine working in conjunction with a crane capable of dealing with loads up to a maximum of 30 tons. In the photograph you will notice that the throat plate has been removed. This is done in order that the copper firebox, to which the foundation ring has now been temporarily secured, may be placed inside the casing.

The foundation ring is of best Yorkshire iron, 4 ins. by $3\frac{3}{4}$ ins. in section, and has to be very accurately machined. The ring is set up on a large milling machine, to which it is secured by duplex jigs so that both the inside and the outside surfaces can be milled with only one setting on the table. The photographs show the ring in the milling machine and on the radial drill.

When the copper box is placed inside the casing the two are correctly lined up in their relative positions and temporarily secured by means of a few crown stays and bolts.

A master template, with numerous indentations forming points of support for the pointed end of a pneumatic portable drilling machine, is fastened along the centre line of the inside box and from this are drilled the stay holes, the drill passing right through the copper and steel plates in order to ensure perfect alignment. The holes are subsequently tapped or screwed ready to receive the large number of stays which are necessary to support the surfaces of the box.

Here is a photograph which gives a very good idea of the appearance of the finished firebox with the throat plate finally riveted in position, and shews the tremendous

Boiler suspended over jaws of hydraulic riveter.

amount of staying that is necessary. The numerous small holes in the copper tube plate are those into which the ends of the small fire tubes are expanded, and the larger holes above them are those into which the ends of the tubes carrying the superheater units are expanded.

Close-up showing size of holes in Tube Plate—
The larger holes are for the Superheater tubes

The barrel is carefully lined up with the firebox, special gauges being used to ensure correct alignment both laterally and vertically. The two parts are temporarily held in position with a few " tacking " bolts before the throat plate connection is drilled ready for riveting in a powerful hydraulic machine having a gap 23 ft. in length, so that the whole boiler unit can be dealt with. An overhead crane, which lifts the boiler into position, is operated from the same platform as the riveting rams. Take a good look at this photograph of the boiler suspended from its crane over the jaws of the hydraulic riveter and lowered between the jaws to complete the riveting around the "connection" and note carefully the size of the boiler compared with the man.

" Foot "-stays and " palm "-stays which are connected to the barrel of the boiler, are then put in and the smokebox tube plate is riveted in position. The tubes are inserted

The Completed Boiler

from the front end of the boiler and the front and back plates are secured by longitudinal steel stays before the boiler is handed over to the boiler mounters for the fitting of the regulator box, superheater, water gauges, safety valves, etc.

When completed the boiler is tested under hydraulic pressure to 290 lbs. per square inch—that is, 40 lbs. per square inch above its working pressure. It is then further tested under steam to a pressure of 250 lbs. per square inch, after which the boiler receives a coat of anti-corrosive paint and it is then ready for handing over to the erecting shop for mounting on the engine frames.

So much then for the construction of the boiler unit, and having got our boiler complete this will simplify the description of the building of the locomotive, which I want to tackle in our next talk.

A " King " in the making, Swindon Works

TALK NUMBER SIXTEEN

BUILDING THE LOCOMOTIVE

Now, with the aid of a good series of photographs, we will try and follow the various stages in the construction of a " King " class engine, and the fact that we have already considered the engine and boiler components should simplify matters for us. We can now turn our attention to the sequence of operations from the placing of the frame plates to the production of the finished engine ready for the road.

We are assuming that all the various parts of the locomotive—those we have considered and many others—have been completed in the respective shops and will come along to the erecting shop as and when required.

The frames, as received from the machine shop, are placed on low trestles with their inner faces uppermost, and on these inner faces are marked the more important locating lines—such as those for the centres of the inside cylinders, inside motion plate, saddle casting, valve gear casting, frame cross stays, and others.

The frames are then turned over bringing the outer surfaces on the top, and these are marked with the centre lines of the outside cylinders, motion plates, and the angle irons which support the footplate. When all this marking has been accurately carried out, the frames are lifted into a vertical position and mounted on adjustable forked stands, six supporting each plate, as it is highly important that, as construction proceeds, the frames shall not sag under the increasing weight which becomes attached to them. Cross-stays are temporarily bolted between the frames to maintain the correct distance apart.

The frames are next tested to ensure that they are dead level, both lengthwise and crosswise. This is done by means of a spirit level, and you will appreciate that the frames must not only be perfectly level, but perfectly square, and, if necessary, one or other of the plates is moved slightly until the diagonal distance between the centres of the leading horn on one side of the engine and of the intermediate horn on the other is exactly the same, whichever pair of opposite horns is taken.

When the frames have been properly squared and levelled, and not until then, is it possible to set up the trailing cheeks of the leading horns. These are the foundations from which other parts of the engine are set, and it is extremely important that they should be correctly fitted. The greatest care is exercised in keeping the cheeks both square and plumb. The other cheeks are set to the trailing cheeks by means of a gauge which ensures that each pair is perfectly parallel.

Perhaps I ought to say again that in locomotives an axle is securely keyed to its pair of wheels. The axles revolve in axleboxes which are in turn housed in " horns " or " cheeks " bolted to the main frames.

It is now possible temporarily to bolt the inside cylinders and motion plate to the frames, the correct position being obtained from lines passing through the bore of the cylinders through the motion plate and over a straight-edge so placed across the frames that one edge (that over which the string line passes) coincides with an imaginary line between the exact centres of the leading horns. Before the holes for the bolts which carry the cylinders and motion casting can be broached out to their finished sizes, the cylinders and motion casting must be set so that they are absolutely central with the " lines," which must themselves be parallel with the top of the frames. The lines must also be at the correct distance from the cheeks of the leading driving horns, and these must be the correct gauge distance from the face of the cylinders.

It is difficult to over-emphasise the importance of the precision necessary in these operations, and in order that these and other lining-up operations may be brought to ever improved standards of perfection, there has recently been installed at Swindon Works an optical lining-up apparatus—the first in Great Britain—which is part of the highly scientific equipment of the "A" erecting shop which we saw on the occasion of our visit to Swindon Works.*

*See " Cheltenham Flyer."

Optical lining-up apparatus in use

Another picture of the optical lining-up apparatus

I should like to give you a detailed description of this ingenious apparatus, but I am afraid it is highly technical. I may say, however, that in addition to providing an accurate means of measuring the alignment of frames and cylinders it also enable precise measurements to be made of the distances from cylinders to driving horn centres, and between driving and other horn centres, all of which are of the utmost importance.

The optical lining-up apparatus comprises a telescope mounted within a tube. The telescope can be pivoted in vertical or horizontal planes by two dials, and when the dials are both set at zero the telescope is in exact central alignment with its external tube. This tube is set by a self-centring spider in the front bell-mouth of one cylinder, and by an adaptor in the stuffing box at the back of the cylinder. A spirit-level ensures that the vertical and horizontal axes are correct, and a measuring surface, set level with the front cylinder face by a straight-edge, provides zero for distance. The overall width across each pair of horns is measured by a vernier, and then a sighting scale is clamped to each horn in turn, and the scale read through the telescope. When these adjustments have been made, the valve gear and saddle castings can be tried in the frames and their positions determined from that of the inside cylinders. The sighting scale is similar to that of a surveyor's staff.

Holes for the carrying bolts are then marked off, the castings are removed for drilling, again inserted in the frames (while holes are broached out), and then temporarily bolted up in order to give the frames sufficient rigidity while the outside cylinders and motion plate are being fitted up. The latter process is very similar to that followed in regard to the inside cylinders, lines being set through to a straight edge across the centres of the intermediate driving horns, and every care taken to ensure that they are square with the frames as well as central with the cylinders and motion plates.

The cheeks of the intermediate driving horns are set from those of the leading driving horns, and here again the greatest care must be exercised in spacing the horns, for this determines the distance between the wheel centres which, in turn, must be rigidly adhered to, for the adoption of coupling rods with solid bushed ends does not permit of any adjustment afterwards. For similar reasons it is essential that the face of the outside cylinders shall be the correct gauge distance from the intermediate driving horns, in this case owing to the solid bushed ends of the outside connecting rods.

With the various angle irons and stays riveted up the framing is practically complete, and as much as possible of the motion work is now added, and such other details as would be exceedingly difficult to undertake after the boiler was in position. The inside cylinder covers are now fitted, together with the motion bars, reversing shafts and brackets, quadrants and auxiliary levers, brake cylinders and reservoirs and, in fact, as much as possible of that which would be more difficult if left till later on.

When all this work has been done, the boiler can be tried on the frames—a sort of first fitting. It is lowered by means of an overhead crane and held loosely in position ready for marking off from the cylinders and saddle castings. The carrying brackets attached to the firebox casing side plates are marked off carefully so as to ensure that the boiler is not only central with the frames transversely, but also that the centre line of the boiler is parallel with the top line of the frames.

There is a second trying on of the boiler, before it is actually secured, in order to check the smokebox holes and mark off on the inside of the carrying bracket the groove which will house the flat bearing springs which are interposed between the frame and the bracket. These springs are about 8 ins. in length, and without them it would be exceedingly difficult to ensure an even distribution of the weight on the frames with such a long firebox as that of the " King " class engines.

Main frames on trestles for marking out.

Two "Kings" under construction: that on right has the inside cylinders in position; that on left has the outside cylinders fitted.

Boiler being lowered between frames by 100 - ton overhead cranes.

Boiler in position ready for fixing to saddle frames

You will probably be surprised to learn that, whilst the boiler is secured at the front end to the cylinder and saddle casting, provision has to be made for expansion under working temperatures, and the back end has, therefore, to be free to slide. The boiler is prevented from lifting at the back by a bracket attached to the frames which fits over the carrying bracket on the boiler.

With the boiler in position a good deal of miscellaneous work can be undertaken, more or less simultaneously. The axle boxes are fitted in the horns and bedded on the axles ; eccentric sheaves and straps are secured in position, and pistons, valves, and crossheads are all assembled.

Boiler covered with non-heat conducting composition.

ngine lifted
r wheeling :
upled wheels
eing placed
to position.

The oiling gear, the exhaust steam grease separator, injector pipe, and other fitments which would be difficult to fix after wheeling, are now added. This work completed, an electric crane with a lifting capacity of 100 tons is brought into operation and the whole structure is raised sufficiently for the six driving wheels to be run underneath and, as the engine is lowered, the axle boxes are guided into the horns. At this stage the front end of the engine is carried on screw jacks, which support the weight of the overhanging end until the bogie can be placed into position.

It is now possible for the coupling and connecting rods to be added and for the valve gear and reversing gear to be

gine lowered
to coupled
eels.

coupled up ready for valve setting. This operation of valve setting is highly important for on the correct distribution of the steam to the cylinders very largely depends the satisfactory running of the engine in service. Before valve

Coating boiler with non-heat-conducting composition

setting is commenced, the screw jacks carrying the front end of the engine are replaced by a dummy bogie which is necessary in order that the engine may be moved backwards and forwards as required while the valve setters are at work.

BUILDING THE LOCOMOTIVE

The valve setting satisfactorily accomplished, a number of other fittings can be added ; springs, cylinder cocks, brake gear, injectors, cab, smokebox, the chimney and many other items which go to make the completed engine, are now secured in their respective positions and the erection of our locomotive is fast approaching finality.

Whilst these many and various additions are being made, the boiler and cylinders are coated with a non-heat-conducting composition of magnesia and asbestos—'white coating' as it is called—and this coating is in turn covered with thin cleating plates of sheet steel.

The handrails are next fitted and as soon as this work is done the painters start operations by removing all grease and dirt from the exterior before applying a " priming " coat to all surfaces which have ultimately to be painted.

Priming is followed by a ' working down ' of the surfaces with " stopping," in order to obtain a smooth surface, and a coat of lead paint is next added. When this has dried, finishing coats of green are applied and the lining out of the barrel, cylinders, etc., is carried out, after which all painted surfaces are given one or more coats of varnish.

While painting is in progress the locomotive is lifted at the front end and the " dummy " bogie is replaced by the bogie proper. When everything is complete, the boiler is filled with water, the locomotive coupled to its tender, and the whole unit is removed from the erecting shop by means of an electric traverser to rails outside.

The next operation is to weigh and level the engine at the correct running height. Weighing is carried out by an ingenious locomotive weighing machine which simultaneously gives the weight on each wheel of the engine, and

Engine on temporary bogie ready for valve setting

Approaching completion : Cab plates fitted. Front of engine lifted to allow bogie to be fixed.

Bogie in position.

Completed Engine being traversed from Erecting Shop to rails outside

the total weight is then distributed over the whole wheel base by a suitable adjustment of the carrying springs.

The new locomotive is now ready for its first run, which is a short trial in order to ascertain if the various parts are functioning correctly, after which any minor adjustments may be made as required.

The engine can then be handed over to the Running Department at Swindon, where it gets a thorough trial in actual service before being passed out to join the fleet of express passenger locomotives.

That, then, is briefly the story of the birth of a " King," and you will all probably be astonished to learn that each of these engines consists of no fewer than 3,500 parts.

1. DAMPER CONTROLS
2. COAL WATERING COCK
3. EXHAUST INJECTOR CONTROL
4. FLAP PLATE
5. FIREHOLE DOORS
6. WATER GAUGE
7. STEAM HEATING PRESSURE GAUGE
8.   „   „   VALVE
9. BOILER STEAM PRESSURE GAUGE
10. EXHAUST INJECTOR LIVE STEAM VALVE
11. RIGHT HAND „   „   „   „
12. VACUUM GAUGE

13. EJECTOR STEAM VALVE
14.   „   AIR   „
15. BLOWER VALVE
16. REGULATOR HANDLE
17. LUBRICATOR
18. REVERSING HANDLE
19. TIP-UP SEAT
20. SANDING GEAR LEVERS
21. AUDIBLE SIGNALLING APPARATUS
22. CYLINDER COCK LEVER

The Cab of a " King " Class Locomotive

TALK NUMBER SEVENTEEN

THE WORKING OF THE LOCOMOTIVE

HAVING followed the development of G.W.R. loco-motives from the earliest days to the present time, and having discussed the various components and their assembly in a modern express passenger engine, we will devote this talk to the working of the locomotive.

You will remember that we covered the ground, some-what briefly, on the occasion of our *Cheltenham Flyer* trip, but today we have the advantage of looking at the subject a little more closely with the aid of this fine coloured diagram* in which the various parts of the engine are numbered and named (below). If you will take the diagram I will, as far as possible, give you the numbers of the various parts as they are mentioned.

We will begin with the fire-box (78) and see what happens there, but first of all just a word or two about fuel. Coal, as you know, is composed principally of carbon, and most of the heat produced from coal is by the combustion of the carbon it contains. When carbon burns it combines with the oxygen from the air.

Now coal is capable of burning in two ways, or rather the oxygen in the air may combine with the carbon in the coal in two ways, depending on the supply of oxygen. If the air is insufficient for complete combustion, each atom of carbon will combine with one of oxygen to

---

*Frontispiece.

form an inflammable gas, carbon monoxide. Should the supply of air be sufficient, each atom of carbon will combine with two of oxygen, forming a non-inflammable gas, carbon dioxide. This is the product of perfect combustion.

Just here, perhaps, I ought to say that the Great Western Railway is fortunate in having within its territory the South Wales coalfields, which produce steam coal of a quality unsurpassed the world over.

When coal is thrown into the fire-box of a locomotive, combustion takes place on the grate in three stages ; first, in the distillation of gases ; secondly, if oxygen is present, these gases are consumed and the oxygen combines with the hydrogen (or hydro-carbons) present; thirdly, the principal constituent, the coke or free carbon, is consumed. These chemical reactions occur gradually, commencing on the surface of the coal with which the heat is in contact, and penetrating, with the heat, until the whole is incandescent. Under practically all conditions a good supply of air should be admitted through the fire-door in order to ensure good combustion, and in this respect the locomotive boiler has an advantage over the stationary boiler on account of the draught created by the blast of the exhaust in the smoke-box. As we have seen, the standard G.W.R. fire-door design embodies provision for a supply of air, even when the doors are closed.

The water in the boiler, as you already know, entirely surrounds the inner fire-box (78) and the outside of the boiler tubes (75). The hot gases from the fire-box pass through the tubes to the smoke box (6) and chimney (1) and in so doing heat the surrounding water.

Now, the effect of heating water is to cause it to expand, and its density is consequently lowered. Thus the water in contact with the fire-box plates on being heated rises, whilst colder streams take its place, to be heated in turn, so setting up a natural circulation of the water in the boiler.

The steam rises to the highest part of the boiler (over the fire-box) and when the regulator handle (63) is moved the regulator valve (12) in the smoke-box is opened and steam which enters the steam pipe (70) by means of the collecting mouth (67), passes to the superheater header (11) and thence to the elements (77), where it is superheated as has already been explained. The superheated steam then passes to each steam chest of the four cylinders, but our diagram can only show the passage to the outside steam chest (14) by way of the internal steam pipe (10), and the outside steam-pipe (9), to between the heads of the piston valve (15).

Just to refresh your mind you might like to look again at the steam chest and cylinder sectional diagram. As you see, the valve heads in the steam chest fit and work in cylindrical bushes or sleeves, and it is between these heads that the live steam enters and outside them that the steam passes from the cylinders (marked " exhaust " in the small diagram) to the blast pipe.

In each of the bushes in the steam chest there is an opening to the corresponding end of the cylinder through which live steam enters and exhaust steam leaves. Entry is only possible when the inside edge of the valve head uncovers the opening, and exit is only possible when the outside edge of the valve head uncovers the same opening.

Now it will, I think, be clear that steam, when admitted to the front end of the cylinder, will force the piston to the back end, and when steam is admitted to the back end of the cylinder, and the steam previously admitted to the front end is permitted to escape, the piston will move forwards.

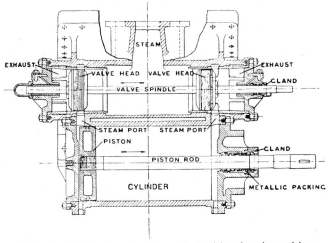

Cylinder Casting shewing steam chest with valves in position

At this point (and while you have the small diagram of the steam chest before you), I want to digress for a moment to tell you of a recent change which has been introduced in regard to the method of securing a steam-tight housing for the valves. As I have said, there is a bush at each end of the steam chest in which the heads of the piston valve work. This bush is renewable and it must obviously be kept steam-tight in the casting. Formerly it was shrunk in, that is, the appropriate portion of the cylinder casting was heated and, when it expanded, the bush was inserted in the casting, which, on contracting as it cooled, gripped and held the bush securely. This method has now been reversed, and instead of heating the cylinder casting, to admit the bush in the temporarily enlarged aperture, the bush is frozen and, in consequence contracts sufficiently for it to be admitted into the untreated casting. The advantages of this change of procedure are a saving of time and more uniform grip of the bush without distortion and subsequent leakage of steam.

So much for the small diagram for the moment, and please look at the large coloured one again. We have got reciprocating, or " to and fro " movement at the piston (17) and consequently to the piston rod (18) attached to it, which passes through the back of the cylinder (26). To the other end of the piston rod is attached a crosshead (31) sliding between two guide bars (34).

The piston head (17), piston rod (18), and crosshead (31) are moved to and fro by steam in the cylinders, and this to and fro motion is converted into rotary motion at the driving wheel (47) by a connecting rod (41) one end of which is secured to the crosshead (31), the other end being fitted to a pin (38) secured in the wheel, a short distance from the axle centre. Pin (38) is called the crank pin and the distance of the crank pin from the centre of the axle is called the " throw " of the crank, which is always exactly one half the stroke of the piston. Thus in the " King " class engine the throw of the crank is 14 ins. and the stroke of the piston (17) is, therefore, 28 ins.

Of the four cylinders, it is impossible in the coloured diagram to show more than the left-hand outside one. The two inside cylinders are supplied with steam from the steam chest (32), and as you know, the piston rods of these cylinders drive the cranked axle of the leading driving wheels (40).

In order to secure an even turning movement on the wheels, the crank pins of the right and left-hand engines of all steam locomotives are set at ninety degrees with each other.

Steam is only admitted into the cylinders for a certain period of the piston stroke, depending upon the setting of the valve gear, which actuates the valves from the movements of the driving axle and the crossheads.

After steam admission to the cylinders, through the port, is cut off by the steam edge of the valve, the steam, by working expansively, continues to exert a gradually decreasing pressure on the piston until the exhaust edge of the valve re-opens the same port, this time to exhaust.

From the cylinders the exhaust steam passes through the blast pipe (7) in the smoke-box (6) and through the chimney (1) to the atmosphere, with every " beat " of the engine. This jet of exhaust steam creates a considerable vacuum in the smoke-box (which you will remember is an air-tight compartment with the exception of the chimney opening), thereby inducing the necessary air draught through the fire.

The purposes of the automatic " jumper top " (13) fitted to the blast pipe (7), the spark arrester and the blower ring (2) were explained when we discussed the smoke-box in which they are all contained.

We had a brief talk about the way in which valves were driven on our *Cheltenham Flyer* trip, and I do not think much more can be added to simplify the explanation of the working of valve gears (unless we are to have a whole series of talks on that rather complicated subject), but you have the diagram of Walschaert's valve gear to help your memory.*

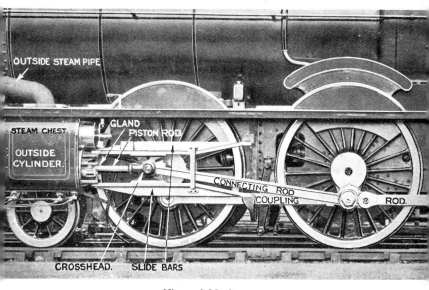

OUTSIDE STEAM PIPE

STEAM CHEST
GLAND
PISTON ROD
OUTSIDE CYLINDER

CONNECTING ROD
COUPLING ROD.

CROSSHEAD.   SLIDE BARS

View of Motion.

The valve gear of all G.W.R. four-cylinder engines is particularly ingenious, as the direct drive to the inside cylinders is through a compensating rocking lever (33), and by this means one set of gear drives two sets of valves.

*See page 168.

If you have studied the coloured diagram carefully you should now, I think, be fairly conversant with the main features of the motive mechanism of a modern railway engine.

◟   ◟   ◟   ◟

So much, then, for the working of the locomotive, and we will conclude this talk with a word or two about the men on the footplate—those who control the working. The locomotive is dependent for performance on the crew which controls it, and inefficiency in the human element may mean ruin to the finest product of locomotive engineering in the world.

Let's see what the engine-driver and fireman do from the time when they arrive at the engine shed and " take over " the engine. Having " booked on " at the time-keeper's office they receive any special instructions for their next run. Since the last trip the shed staff have coaled, cleaned, and watered the locomotive, and any small adjustments rendered necessary have been made by the shed staff.

Driver and fireman take over their engine as it stands in the running shed over one of the inspection pits. The fire has already been lighted and steam pressure shows about 60 lbs. per square inch.

The driver proceeds to go thoroughly over the engine oiling up and examining the motion, etc., while the fireman tests his water gauge cocks, observes the water level in the boiler and checks his equipment, that is shovel, fire-irons, tools, lamps, detonators, red flags, etc. He then examines the smoke-box to see that the spark plate and

On the Footplate

jumper top (13) are in good order and that the smoke-box door (5) is close fitting, otherwise the draught will be impaired and this will affect the steaming of the boiler. He also examines the ashpan (52) and dampers (54) and, if necessary, he then proceeds to get up steam more quickly by using the blower (2) operated from the cab in order to get sufficient pressure to test the injectors.

In due course the locomotive leaves its place over the pit in the Running Shed. It is " turned " on the engine turn-table, and then proceeds tender first to its train of coaches waiting at the station platform.

On arrival the engine backs on to the train to which it is coupled by the fireman, who afterwards examines and re-arranges his lamps. He waters the coal, which not only lays the dust, but also prevents fine coal from being drawn through the tubes (75) before becoming ignited. While waiting, the steam pressure rises gradually and the fireman endeavours to prevent it escaping at the safety valve (71) by using it in his injector to feed the boiler with water.

Just before departure time, the guard of the train will come along and report to the driver the number, type, and weight of vehicles on the train and inform him of any special notices affecting the trip.

This done, driver and fireman await the starting signal, and soon after the shrill whistle of the guard is heard from the rear of the train giving the " right-away."

The driver, having previously moved the reversing handle (61) to " full forward gear " ready for the start, glances at the vacuum gauge to make sure all brakes are off and, providing the starting signal is " off," blows his whistle (65). He then opens the cylinder cocks (25) by means of the lever (56) and slightly moves the regulator valve handle (63) to admit steam to the steam chests and, after a few turns of the wheels, closes the cylinder cocks through which has been blown any steam which may have been condensed in the cylinders.

The engine starts gently, but soon gathers speed and the driver then adjusts the reversing gear (61) so that the piston valves (15) will restrict the openings from the steam chests (14) to the cylinders (26), thereby admitting less steam and making use of its expansive action.

The driver then moves the regulator handle (63) to " full open " position, and all this time is keeping a keen eye open for signals.

Meanwhile his fireman is alternately working the injectors to keep up the supply of water in the boiler and shovelling coal through the firehole door (62) in order to maintain the burning mass of fuel required to generate the steam which the engine is demanding.

When the train is well on the run, the driver further adjusts his reversing gear (61) so as to work his engine still more economically in steam, and the two men can then settle down to their job.

You may possibly be surprised to learn that even during a long run very little conversation passes between driver and fireman unless, of course, something untoward happens, and even then their remarks are exceedingly brief. For one thing the noise makes conversation difficult, but while on the run both men on the footplate have their attention fully occupied with their respective jobs. The driver's eyes are almost fixed at the look-out window and his hand is never far from the regulator. Complete understanding of his engine enables him to judge just where to shut off steam and apply his brakes so as to bring the train to a stop at precisely the right spot under varying conditions of load, weather, etc.

The driver must be well acquainted with the booked timing of his train (as given in the " working " timetable) so that he may pass, or stop at places *en route*, at the scheduled times. The " working " or " service " timetable differs considerably from that issued to the public, and besides giving the times of arrival and departure for all stations, etc., at which a train stops, it also gives the " passing " times for certain stations, junctions, signal boxes, etc.

The fireman is kept constantly busy in feeding the fire and the boiler. At certain points on the run he also operates handle (101) which controls the apparatus (95, 96) by which water is picked up from troughs laid between the rails, when the train is running at speed.

Whilst his principal duty is, of course, to see that the driver has sufficient steam at his command at all stages of the journey, you must not think that the fireman's know-ledge of the locomotive is confined to the boiler. Like the driver, he has started his career as an engine cleaner, but he has also been firing on shunting engines, and less important trains, before graduating to the footplate of an express passenger train, during which he has learned a good deal about the practical working of the various parts of the locomotive. In addition to such practical experience he has also attended classes and received instruction from others, aided by models and drawings in the theory of locomotive working.

The driver has passed through all stages of firing before being graded as an engine driver, and he has had to work his way up from shunting engine driver, branch passenger train engine, goods train engine, etc., to the highest position, namely, the control of an express passenger train.

Drivers and firemen are divided up into what are termed " links," according to the class of engine, the different trains to be worked, and also the seniority of the men. The senior drivers and firemen as a rule work the express passenger trains with the large express engines, a link being formed of a sufficient number of men and engines to cope with the number of express trains to be run.

Locomotive drivers and firemen must have sound health, keen eyesight, and good hearing. To be the driver of an express passenger train locomotive is, of course, the ultimate objective of every cleaner, fireman, and driver, and the men who graduate to these positions are worthy of their high calling which is one demanding a sense of responsibility, a steady nerve, and cool judgment.

It would be ungracious, indeed, to breathe a word against those celebrities who lend lustre to our school speech-days by distributing (chiefly to the other fellows) book rewards for prowess in study. Having succeeded in life, they, perhaps not unnaturally, elect to enlighten us as to their youthful ambitions, but it is a little difficult to appreciate why they expect to raise a smile by stating that they once yearned to be railway engine-drivers. This would-be-engine-driver story is wearing almost as threadbare as our American visitors' " Your policemen are wonderful ! " Besides, we do not even know that these " highbrows," who regard the engine-driving ambition as so amusing, would ever make a good job of it.

A Contrast—A Century's Progress.

TALK NUMBER EIGHTEEN

CONCLUSION

U NFORTUNATELY the pioneers who constructed the first railways did not, and perhaps, could not, envisage the vast potentialities of the system they founded. It is probably true to say that even the prophetic vision of Brunel hardly foresaw the five hundred tons load of a modern high speed passenger train, or the freight train with double that weight behind the locomotive tender.

The need for the giant locomotives we know today was not anticipated a century ago, and in providing the amount of space required for the original tracks, and in making the tunnels, bridges, and other structures, allowance was not made for larger engines, etc. Consequently the locomotive engineer of today has to build his engines to limitations largely imposed by the railway pioneers of the early nineteenth century. Pioneering, you see, may have its disadvantages.

You have already made the acquaintance of the load gauge,* and will be able to understand how the limitations it imposes confine the locomotive engineer to close dimensions. We have seen how the power of the locomotive has continued to increase to meet the demands of heavier and still heavier trains. Now, of course, heavier

---

*See " Track Topics."

trains require more power to haul them, that means bigger cylinders, which in turn mean bigger boilers to provide more steam : the result is much bigger and much heavier engines. If you compare some of the photographs of early locomotives with those of today, the increase in the size of the boilers will be at once apparent.

While those early locomotives had small boilers, they also had high chimneys, and it is a good job they had, otherwise the loading gauge might have been even more restricted than it is, for the bridges over the line, tunnels, etc., were built to accommodate those old time engines with their high chimneys. As the boilers have become bigger, the chimneys have become smaller, and today we get the squat but business-like chimneys of the *Kings* and *Castles* and the huge boilers built almost up to the limits of the gauge.

Though locomotives can only expand within certain limits in width and height, there is another dimension which does not impose quite the same drastic restriction, i.e., length, but here again the locomotive engineer is confronted by the limits imposed by curves in the track, for you can well understand that the distance between which the wheels are spaced becomes a factor for consideration as does also, among other things, the size of existing turn-tables.

Another limitation is that of weight, and weight is a most important factor. The load that can be safely carried on certain tracks, and particularly on under-bridges, must be limited, and as the height of an over-bridge limits the size of the locomotive, so the strength of under-bridges must govern the weights of the locomotives passing over them.

When passing over a bridge, the weight of the loco-motive must be distributed evenly over a number of axles,

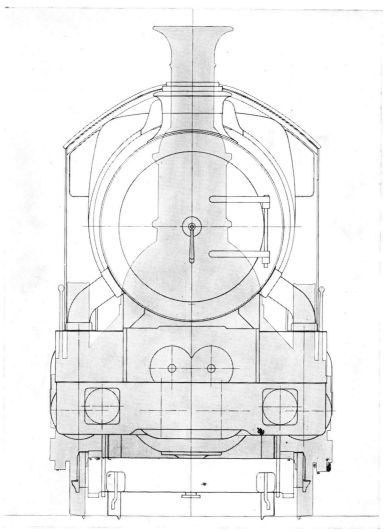

A contrast in outline—" North Star " and " King " Class Locomotive

and for many years 20 tons was regarded as the limit per axle in this country. The load carried on the coupled driving axles of the " King " class engine has been increased to 22½ tons, and you can readily appreciate why the use of these giant locomotives must necessarily be restricted to

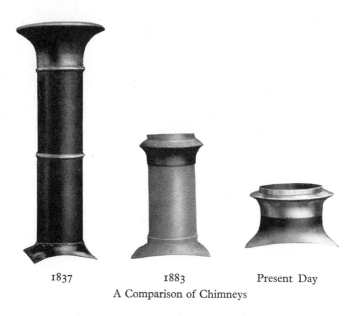

| 1837 | 1883 | Present Day |

A Comparison of Chimneys

main line working, and why the heavy types of engines can only work over subsidiary portions of the railway after the necessary strengthening of the track and bridges has been carried out.

You will now, I think, begin to realise what the locomotive engineer is up against in the matter of restrictions and why in countries like Canada and the United States of America, which built their main line railways later and profited by the experience of this and other countries, the locomotives are so much bigger and more powerful. In this connection you must also remember that,with so much mileage in open country where level crossings are common and bridges comparatively rare, many restrictions experienced by the British locomotive engineer do not arise.

But difficulties are made to be overcome, and our locomotive engineers are out to solve the problem of the restrictions imposed by the load gauge. When I tell you that some twenty years ago there was serious talk of the steam railway locomotive having reached its maximum size and power, you will be able to appreciate that, in locomotive engineering as in other spheres, the problems of doing what it is said cannot be done, are being successfully tackled. You have only to compare Great Western Railway engines of the pre-war era with those of today for proof of the continuous development that has taken place in the steam railway locomotive since it was stated to have reached the limits of size and power.

∽　∽　∽　∽

And what of the future of the steam locomotive ? Well, that is a difficult question to answer in a few words—or in many words for that matter.

Fools in their folly have said that the death knell of the steam locomotive was sounded with the coming of electric traction, while others were equally sure about its sudden demise when the first diesel-engined rail-motor appeared.

At the very birth of the railways there were Jeremiahs who proved (to their own satisfaction) that the locomotive was either a weakling which could not survive, or a monster of destruction which would not let anything else survive.

The modern steam railway locomotive is no upstart. It has been tried and proved and consistently improved over a hundred years and, as you know, it boasts a noble and distinguished ancestry.

It certainly seems difficult to imagine our steel highways *without* steam locomotives, for despite the attractions and the wonders of aeronautics, electricity, and ' wireless ' and the rapid development of the internal combustion engine in its many spheres, the steam railway locomotive continues to hold first place in the affection and esteem of " boys of all ages." I was going to say ' reverence,' and perhaps it is not putting it too high to say that as long as there have been railway locomotives they have not lacked youthful admirers who regard the cab of an express passenger engine as something akin to a " holy of holies " and the occupants of the footplate as " little lower than the angels."

It has been said that there are people who fail to be fascinated or intrigued by a modern express locomotive, but surely that is difficult to believe. The steam engine is the glory of our railways as it is of the Navy and Mercantile Marine, and no usurper of its place can hope to command the same veneration.

It is doubtful if any mechanised vehicle has the same attraction as a modern steam railway locomotive, for where can we find such an embodiment of grace, strength, speed, and pent-up power—sufficient to draw a train of five hundred tons at speeds reaching 80 miles an hour for hundreds of miles ?

CONCLUSION

There may, of course, be all sorts of " ſtuffy," or even scientific, reasons why the railway ſteam locomotive should ultimately give place to some other form of tractive power, but let us hope that its passing is not yet.

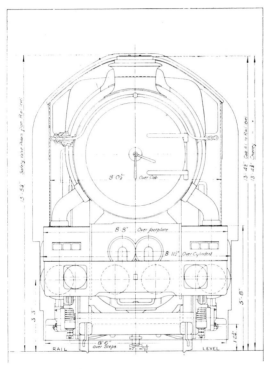

Our railways, which are the envy of the whole world, remember, have been built up on ſteam locomotion. During the hundred odd years of their exiſtence in this country—the country which gave railways to the world—

"Wheels of Industry"—A visit to Swindon Locomotive Works

CONCLUSION

the locomotive has developed from Stephenson's small four wheeled engine weighing less than seven tons, to wonderfully powerful, speedy, and efficient giants of ten wheels weighing a hundred tons and over, such as the famous *Kings*, *Castles*, etc.

There are in this country over twenty thousand steam locomotives, so that if they do receive sentence of death, it is going to be a pretty big funeral. One thing is quite certain, there will be hundreds of thousands of sincere mourners.

It is probably true that with the production of very cheap electricity—far cheaper than is at present generally available—schemes for the electrification of some further sections of our railways, particularly suburban passenger lines, may result, but wholesale electrification would take a good many years and many, many, millions of pounds to accomplish, and it may well be that long before any system of electrification could be generally adopted, a better or more economical one might be evolved. There are other alternatives, too, and one is that the steam locomotive itself may be capable of still further improvement along entirely new lines, and in saying this I must add quite frankly that the wish fathers the thought.

The steam locomotive is a self-contained machine. It generates its own energy and is not dependent upon a distant station for its power. With the steam system the motive power is distributed over many units, so that should one engine fail it can be quickly replaced. With an electrified system, however, a failure of motive power might quickly bring all trains in that area or system to a stand. Decentralisation of motive power has many advantages.

The steam system has served us well, and it is far too valuable to scrap, without very careful consideration of all

West of England Express hauled by "King" Class locomotive *King Edward VIII*

the " pros and cons," and they are, indeed, many. But apart altogether from economic and such like considerations the electric locomotive simply hasn't got the same personality. It can never take the place of the steam engine in our affections, nor can it appeal to us in the same way. After all, what is a thing of switches, taps, and knobs, taking its power from some distant source, compared with the engine which raises its own steam and is as responsive to the demands of its driver and fireman as a horse is to its rider ?

Long may the railway locomotive steam !

But let us hear a higher authority on this matter. Listen to what Sir Robert Horne, the Chairman of the Great Western Railway, has to say on this subject :—

". . . . . let nobody imagine that the days of the steam locomotive are done or even declining. No railway company in the world has more successfully proved its capacity for regular running with heavy loads at very high rates of speed than the Great Western, and we shall probably demonstrate this fact with even more emphasis before long. We aspire always to keep the best of the past while neglecting no opportunity or device which will enable us to advance in the future."

After that assurance we can quite safely leave it to the Company which was running motor 'buses in Cornwall before they appeared upon the streets of London, and which inaugurated the first railway air service, to maintain its foremost position in the matter of railway locomotive progress.

Don't *you* think so ?

A U   R E V O I R

Companion Railway Books

In the Popular G.W.R. "Boys of All Ages" Series
By W. G. CHAPMAN.

One
Shilling
Each

CHELTENHAM FLYER
A NEW RAILWAY BOOK FOR BOYS
OF ALL AGES.

240 pages   140 Illustrations
Folding Coloured Frontispiece

The story of Great Britain's Fastest
Steam Train is brimful of fascinating
facts and " how-it-works " descrip-
tions of Locomotives, Coaches, Signals, Automatic Train Control,
Track Equipment, and all the intriguing mechanism and methods of
a modern railway.

" Cheltenham Flyer " has met
with an enthusiastic reception by
railway enthusiasts the World over,
and three large editions were demanded within six months of publication.

"Has YOUR Boy got HIS Copy?"

TRACK TOPICS
A BOOK OF RAILWAY ENGINEERING
FOR BOYS OF ALL AGES.

260 pages   168 *Illustrations*
Photogravure Frontispiece

" Track Topics " is concerned
with the railway track and its
structures—tunnels, cuttings, em-
bankments, viaducts, bridges, etc.

The text of the book consists of
twenty descriptive " talks " which
explain the problems confronting
Brunel, the famous first Engineer
of the Great Western Railway, in
making his railway to the West,
describe modern methods of construction and maintenance of the
steel highway, and explain how it
is taken over and under roads and
rivers, through hills and across
valleys, etc.

"Get on the track of 'Track Topics.' "

*The publications of the Great Western Railway are obtainable from
G.W.R. Stations or Offices, Railway Bookstalls, Agencies, Book-
sellers, or direct from the Superintendent of the Line, G.W.R.,
Paddington Station, London, W.2.*

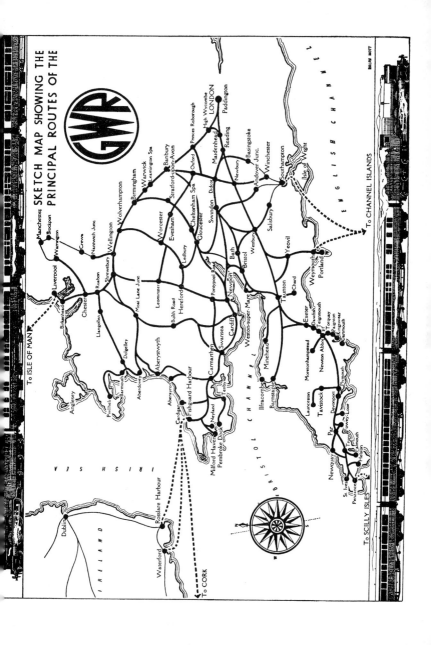

SKETCH MAP SHOWING THE
PRINCIPAL ROUTES OF THE